KU-274-258

PROGRESSIVE BADMINTON

PROGRESSIVE BADMINTON

by

KEN CROSSLEY

Chief Coach
Badminton Association of England

LONDON: G. BELL AND SONS LTD

Copyright © 1970 by
G. BELL AND SONS LTD
York House, Portugal Street
London, WC2A 2HL

All rights reserved. No part of this publication may be
reproduced, stored in a retrieval system, or transmitted,
in any form or by any means, electronic, mechanical,
photocopying, recording or otherwise, without the prior
permission of the Copyright owner.

First published 1970
Reprinted 1975

156394

JAMES GRAHAM COLLEGE
OF EDUCATION LIBRARY
CHAPEL LANE, FARNLEY, LEEDS

8 MAR 1976

CLASS No: 796·345

ACC. No: 50462

170410863.

LEEDS POLY

350462

V

796·345

ISBN 0 7135 1940 1

Printed in Great Britain by
The Camelot Press Ltd, Southampton

Acknowledgments

A great many people, over the years, have unwittingly helped me to write this book, but I would like to thank particularly the following for their more direct and immediate assistance:

The International Badminton Federation for permission to print the Laws of the Game.
Jackie Hammond for her invaluable typing.
Graham Habbin who allowed me to use his fine action pictures of games during the All-England Championships and who photographed the strokes illustrated.
Alison Watson, Helen Crossley, Peter Gardner and Garry Roberts who posed for these photographs.
The Coca-Cola Company for permission to use photographs taken at the London Championships.
Nancy Horner who inspired me to write the book and who patiently gave me invaluable help and advice.

Contents

	Page
Introduction	9

Part One: MAKING A START

How to Start Playing	12
Scoring	13
Equipment: The Shuttlecock, The Racket, What to Wear	16

Part Two: BASIC TECHNIQUES

The Grip	23
The Wrist Action	27
Footwork	29

Part Three: THE STROKES

The Service, The Flick Service, The High Service, The Drive Service	37
Return of Service	46
The Overhead Forehand Strokes	50
The Overhead Backhand Strokes	55
The Drives	60
Underarm Strokes	63
Net Shots	66
Return to a Smash	69
Round-the-Head	70

Part Four: TACTICS

Singles	78
Mixed Doubles	86
Men's Doubles	102
Ladies' Doubles	113
To Conclude	119
Appendix: The Laws of Badminton	120

Introduction

Once upon a time man started to play badminton. I am not sure when, for the exact origins of the game are shrouded in mystery, although there is little doubt that it evolved from battledore and shuttlecock which was played in England in the 17th century, and there is evidence that a game similar to badminton was played much earlier in China.

The name is derived from the seat of the Duke of Beaufort at Badminton in Gloucester where the game is supposed to have been played about 1870 by army officers, guests of the Duke, home on leave from India. These sporting gents took this new activity back to India with them, where, in 1887, the first rules were formulated.

But enough of the history. Let it suffice to say that from very crude beginnings has emerged a highly efficient, energetic sport with getting on for half a million people taking part in it in this country alone. It is also encouraging to note that more and more schoolchildren are taking an interest in the game and I think it is true to say that most schools in England have introduced badminton to their children, either as an extra-curricula activity, or even as an actual class activity. I was interested to note, when I re-read Eddie Choong's book recently, that he said in 1953, 'In schools, badminton has made little progress. Court accommodation is difficult, and the price of expendable shuttlecocks a bar.' He would certainly have to change his opinion today and I know that no one would be more ready to do so than Eddie. Despite all the difficulties, badminton is forging ahead. Obstacles are being overcome. Enlightened education authorities are, whenever possible, ensuring that any new schools and sports halls erected are capable of supporting badminton, and I am sure that in the near future we shall see more and more school halls being thrown open to the public for their participation in the game.

This upsurge is not restricted to England alone. When the International Badminton Federation was founded in 1934, 9 countries were founder members. In 1954 the number had risen to 24 and today 51 national associations are affiliated. These developments have naturally fostered a high degree of international rivalry and so, through the years, an increasing number of international fixtures have been arranged. Quite apart from the obvious benefits to be derived from these exchanges they have brought new thinking into the game. In the early days, badminton was very much a social recreation, but today, at the highest level, it is a very serious sport and its recent inclusion in the Empire Games, for the first time, bears proof of this.

However, it may well be that you do not seek the champion's laurels. Badminton is, above all, a game to be enjoyed. Even if you wished to become a champion, you could not do so unless you really enjoyed playing the game. But I do believe that the better one can perform at any game, the more enjoyment can be derived from it. It is with this thought in mind that I have written this book. If you are just starting out I hope to guide you along the right path, so that you can make rapid improvement without getting into some of those bad habits which often prove so difficult to correct at a later date. If you have already been introduced to the game, then there is something here for you as well, to advance your game further and perhaps take up the competitive play you have been thinking about. Even if you are an experienced player there may be some advantage to you in reading these pages. I may just say something you hadn't thought of!

I would recommend that, first of all, you read this book through from beginning to end, and then go back to study more deeply the aspect of the game with which you are currently concerned. The book is not intended to guarantee success, because that can be achieved only by determined effort. However, if you are sensible in your approach and and pick out the sections which concern your weakness and work on your weakness diligently, you must succeed.

Do not attempt to do too much at once. Try one or two techniques at a time, but leave the more advanced ones until you really feel ready for them. I lay great stress on the basics and I entreat you to follow my advice. The advanced play will come, believe me, but it will come all the sooner if you can get the fundamentals right first.

No matter what your age, sex, or level of play may be, it will be an advantage if you can work with a partner equally keen to improve. Practice together and do not be afraid to criticise each other. A spot of friendly competition is healthy and will do you both good.

To avoid repetition I have assumed that you are a right-handed player, but if you are not, you must naturally substitute 'left' for 'right' where appropriate. For the same reason I refer to you and others as males except where the context obviously refers to the fair sex.

To some players, badminton becomes almost a religion. You may not think that this applies to you. But, no matter what your aim may be, remember it is a game to be enjoyed and I sincerely hope that this book will help towards that end.

Part One: MAKING A START

HOW TO START PLAYING

Take one shuttlecock, one racket and a kindred spirit similarly armed and hit the shuttlecock back and forth to each other. If you can carry out this simple task, then you can play badminton. True, your rallies are a long way removed from what you may have seen at the All-England Championships, but remember, the champions looked and felt very much like you when they first picked up a badminton racket.

Obviously, I cannot tell why you have decided to learn to play badminton. It may be just for some exercise or perhaps you are interested in a recreational activity with a good sociable background. Or, it may be that you believe that this game could improve or maintain your fitness for some other sport in which you participate. Badminton can do all these things, but the first essential is that you must enjoy it. Later on, perhaps, you may decide that you could go a long way in badminton and, if this should prove to be the case, I hope that this book will have helped to smooth your path.

It is often said that we learn by our mistakes, but, whilst this is true, I would rather say that we learn by our successes. Anyone who has experienced that glorious moment when a perfectly timed backhand clear has sent the shuttle soaring high into the air to land smack on the base line will know what I mean. To feel success in anything is the best teacher I know.

Well, let us start along the badminton road, even though you will not necessarily know where you are going. I must warn you that there are going to be hold-ups and delays and there will be times when you will feel that you have travelled far enough. So be it, the decision will be yours and I shall be content just so long as I can see you are having fun playing this great game.

Like all good travellers, we must know before commencing our journey something about the terrain we are to cover and familiarise ourselves with the equipment we shall have to use. I take it that you have at least a rough idea of what badminton is all about and that you know that it is a game played between either two players (singles) or four players (doubles) on a rectangular court, divided exactly in half by a net 5 feet high. The players use a racket to strike a shuttlecock (which may only be struck whilst in the air before it touches the ground,) backwards and forwards over a net in an endeavour either to hit it on to the floor in the opponent's half of the court, or to force the opponent to hit it out of play.

Naturally, badminton has Laws governing the game and you will find these printed in full on page 120. I think that you should read these, for they are neither numerous nor difficult, with the possible exception of the scoring which you may find confusing at first. We shall cover some of the main Laws as we go along. Also on page 124 there is a diagram of a court which shows the dimensions, the markings and the names given to the areas and the lines bounding the court. You should study this as soon as possible.

SCORING

Scoring does sometimes present a problem to the beginner, but you will find that it is really quite easy and you will have no difficulty once you have played a few games. However, let me see if I can simplify it for you. I think it would be easier if we considered the singles game first: that is, one player against one other player, or, you against me. To decide who serves first, we would usually spin a racket and one of us would call 'rough' or 'smooth'. Let us say that I spun the racket and that you called 'rough' and the racket fell rough side up. That is, the side where the trimming strings appear underneath the main strings of the racket. You would have won the toss and by so doing you would have the choice of (a) serving first, (b) not serving first, or, (c) choice of the side of court you will occupy in the first game. If you choose (a), I would have choice of ends, i.e. (c). However if you chose (b), I would not only have choice of ends but I would also serve first.

When starting off a game of badminton, the first service must always be delivered from the right-hand service court, diagonally across into the receiver's right-hand service court. If you serve to me but fail to win the rally, the service comes to me. But, if you do win the rally, while you are serving, you score a point and you serve again. Your next service would be from the left-hand court, diagonally across into the left-hand court and, if you win this rally, you score another point and your third service would be from the right-hand service court again. The most important thing to remember about scoring in badminton is that *you only score points when you are serving*.

For instance, if you serve to me and I fail to win the rally, since you are the server, you score one point *and* serve again. Then, you will continue to serve until you commit a fault. As soon as you fail to make a good return the service passes to me, but I do not win a point because you were serving. I merely win the right to serve and I must win a rally while I am serving, in order to win a point myself. And so the game continues, remembering to change from the right court to the left court as the scores alter. It is the server's score which decides from which court the service will be delivered. For example, when the server's score is an even number, 0–2–4–, etc., the service would be from the right-hand court and when the server's score is odd, 1–3–5–, etc., it will be from the left. In badminton, a score of nothing is called 'love' and the server's score is always mentioned first.

The men's singles and all the doubles games consist of 15 points (although in certain cases 21 may be allowed) whilst the ladies' singles game is 11 points. A match is the best of three games. When a game is tied at 13-all or 14-all in doubles or men's singles or 9-all or 10-all in ladies' singles, the player who first reaches the score may 'set' the game. For this feature would you refer to Law 7 which sets out the position very clearly.

In doubles play the procedure and scoring is very similar except, of course, allowance must be made for the four players now on court. The two players who at the moment hold the service are called the 'IN' side and their opponents the 'OUT' side. Only one player of the side beginning a game is entitled to serve in its first innings and he will play, just as he did in singles, by delivering his first service from the right-hand court to the opposing right-hand court and then, if he wins the rally his second service from the left-hand court and so on. When his side loses a rally, on this first time round, the service passes to the opponents. From then on both players on each side have a chance to serve when their side is the 'IN' side.

The courts which you or your partner *must* occupy when *serving* or *receiving service* are dictated by your sides' score. If, at the beginning of the game, you occupied the right-hand court and your partner the left, then if your side's score is even you will serve or receive from the right-hand court. If your side's score is odd, it is your partner who will serve or receive from the right-hand court and, of course, exactly the same principle applies to services delivered and received from the left-hand court. Laws 9 to 12 cover in detail the doubles play, but please do not worry about it. As I said before, it will all become second nature to you after only a short while. Once the shuttle is in play there is no question of anyone *having* to occupy any given area, indeed the players *must* be prepared to move all over the court.

THE SHUTTLECOCK

The outstanding feature of the game of badminton is the shuttlecock—or shuttle or 'bird' as it is more frequently called. The unique construction of the shuttle, which weighs only one-sixth of an once, provides the reason for most of badminton's appeal. Many people erroneously believe that the flight of the shuttle is erratic. This is not so, for a shuttle will always act in the same manner when struck at the same force and at the same angle. A hard-hit shuttle leaves the racket at considerable speed and as long as this speed is maintained it travels in a straight line. But, at a certain point in its flight, the speed decreases rapidly, the shuttle turns, base downwards and falls almost perpendicularly. It is this characteristic that the experienced player uses for a basic strategy of his game. It is the peculiar make-up of the badminton shuttle that makes it possible, in one shot, for the shuttle to leave the racket at speeds over 100 m.p.h. and with the very next shot for the player almost to make the shuttle 'sit up and beg'.

The most widely used shuttlecocks are made from specially selected goose feathers, 14–16 in number, inserted into a kid-covered cork base. Naturally, there are various grades of quality but most players prefer to use the best quality as these generally speaking are more durable and in the long run cost little more than the cheaper variety. So carefully are these top quality 'feathered' shuttles made that they can be graded by weight from 73 to 85 grains. This is most important, for the greater the weight, the faster and further will the shuttle fly and this means that by selecting the correct weight you can always have the correct shuttle to use on your court. See Laws of Badminton No. 4 for testing shuttles. This is accurate and simple to perform, and will ensure that you obtain the very best performance from the shuttle as well as extending its life.

Because the feathered shuttles are so delicate in construction they are naturally quite expensive and even with the greatest care they have a very short life expectancy. Therefore the development of a synthetic shuttle has been attended by a keen interest, particularly amongst the small, one-court clubs to whom rising costs have been a tremendous handicap. Despite a very cool initial reception and perhaps a rather stormy passage over the last twenty years, I think it is now true to say that the best quality 'plastic' bird competes favourably with its feathered counterpart. Of course you will still find certain players, particularly amongst the top-liners, who maintain that the feathered shuttle has more 'feel' than the plastic, but I doubt whether the average club player would notice any difference to his game and I think the size of your pocket will be the determining factor.

THE RACKET

Curb the impulse to go straight out and buy yourself a racket, instead, if this is possible, try to use those of your friends for the odd game. A badminton racket is an expensive item and, obviously, the most vital part of your equipment. During your playing career there is a very good chance that you will try many rackets, and as you gain experience I am sure you will come to the same conclusion as myself, which is that there is nothing to choose between the top rackets of the leading manufacturers. What is of paramount importance is that you choose one which suits you. As you go along you will learn that a badminton racket is not just a lump of wood stuck in your hand: it becomes a part of you, an extension to your arm. This sensation can only be felt if the racket is of perfect dimensions and, above all, perfect balance *for you*.

The Laws of the game do not lay down any specifications for rackets, but over the years the racket makers have created

their products on a standard pattern to roughly the same
dimensions. The usual length is 26 in. with an oval head 10
in. by 8 in. Of recent years, due to pressure from the top
players, the weight of rackets has decreased and modern
manufacturing technique has now made it possible to con-
struct very light, but still very strong, models. The average
weight is 5 oz. or just under, although a racket produced by
one firm weighs under 4 oz.

It is quite impossible for me to recommend a particular
model to suit you, but I do think the old adage 'you get what
you pay for' holds good. I would always advocate that you go
for the best you can afford. When you do purchase a racket,
pay particular attention to the grip and ensure that you
choose one that is the right size for your hand, one you can
grasp comfortably, without feeling any strain on the fingers,
and manipulate easily. Swish it about to see that it has a bit
of whip and does not feel too heavy in the head for you. A
champion racket will not necessarily make you a champion
but it should make life easier for you. However, no matter
what you do buy, please remember that it is a delicate
instrument and must be treated as such. If the racket head
is made of laminated wood, a press is absolutely essential,
but if you have an all-steel frame model a press is not
necessary. In either event, when not in use, the racket should
be kept in a dry but cool atmosphere.

Some models will offer a choice of natural gut or synthetic
strings and I am afraid that you will find that gut is more
expensive. Equally, as the quality of the synthetic material
decreases so does the price. I prefer gut myself for I believe
it has more 'life' and it is more responsive to the finer strokes
but, as a rule, I would recommend a good quality synthetic
for the beginner, mainly from an expense point of view.
Apart from the initial cost, synthetic should last longer and
should not break as frequently as gut on the mis-hits—
which are bound to happen quite regularly in the early
days of learning the game.

WHAT TO WEAR

A tradition has grown up in badminton that only white clothing should be worn on court, and indeed in the majority of tournaments a regulation to this effect is imposed as a condition of entry. Until quite recently, track suits of any colour were banned, but in most events today, white track suits are permitted, *though only for the initial knock-up*. I do not think that the majority of badminton players are too concerned with sartorial elegance, for their choice of clothing is determined largely by common sense. If you play this game hard you will get hot, and I am sure you will agree that it is undesirable to come, play and go home in the same kit. You can imagine the result of perspiring in a navy-blue shirt or red pullover. In short, there is a lot to be said for always changing to play, and there are decided benefits in your clothes being white as you will need to wash them often!

Nevertheless, I know from bitter experience how miserable it can feel to walk on to a freezing court in mid-winter with only a pair of shorts as my nether garments and I, for my part, would never object to seeing players in track suits if the temperature so dictated. However, be that as it may, a great deal of fast movement can be necessary in badminton and shorts, or, in the case of ladies, skirts, are really the best garments for allowing freedom of movement. When you join a club, see what the custom is and follow that. But if the hall where you play is at all cold, I strongly recommend that you do something to keep your legs warm at least in between games. It is a most dangerous practice to run around making sudden, jerky movements with cold limbs.

A purpose made, white, sports shirt is a sound investment. The modern nylon or drip-dry shirt can be quite uncomfortable if you get hot and tend to perspire.

The correct shoes for the game are very important. Most clubs, particularly if they have a light-coloured floor, will insist on the soles of the shoes being of a material which will not mark. This feature will take you out of the cheap bracket,

but even if it were not so I would not advise you to skimp on
your footwear. Go for a good pair of shoes which have been
specially designed for the job. The manufacturers have had a
lot of experience and over the years have discovered just
where they should be reinforced or padded. Look carefully at
the soles to ensure you will have a good grip on the floor and,
obviously, make quite sure they are a good fit.

There are some excellent socks on the market today, usually fairly thick, specially made for the job in hand and these,
if not cheap, should prove to be a valuable purchase.

A sweater or cardigan is a must for badminton during the
winter months. You will want to wear it during the knock-
up and the easy part of the game and certainly it will be
invaluable for wear in between games. Again, a good quality
garment should prove the better buy in the long run.

I think the only other immediate item of equipment you
need consider is a bag of some sort to carry your clothing
around in. There are many on the market to choose from
and although it need not be capable of holding your racket as
well, you will find it useful to have all your gear together.

Now that you are prepared for the journey you will need
a passport. Whilst it is true that just you and one friend could
play badminton, after a while you would find this mono-
tonous; besides you might find it difficult in your area to
hire a court for casual games, and so you should join a club.
Apart from the social aspect you will find that playing with
different people and watching their way of doing things will
greatly assist your own development. I am sure there must be
a club in your area and the majority of clubs will welcome
new members, providing you know a little bit about the
game.

If you are an absolute beginner you may run into a snag
when you join a club, particularly if that club does not have
special arrangements to cater for 'rabbits': that is that there
is no one prepared to take you on one side and show you the

best way to learn or to improve your game. If you are an
absolute beginner and you can't find a club which caters for
you and you are embarrassed at thrusting yourself on your
betters, I would recommend that you find a friend in the same
boat and if at all possible hire a court together. In some areas
it is possible to join an evening institute where you can
obtain coaching as well as play and this could be a valuable
stepping-stone to a club.

For Part Two of the book I have made the assumption that
you can control the shuttlecock well enough to play a
simple rally and that you will have the facilities to put into
practice what I preach.

Part Two: BASIC TECHNIQUES

Most of us try to run before we can walk and you are probably no exception. I am sure you are anxious to develop a full range of the strokes used in badminton and it may well be that you are a born 'natural' who, without very much conscious effort, can do just that. However, unless you are one of these fortunate beings, you will find that although you understand what you are supposed to be doing, a shot just does not come off as it should. This probably means that there is some fault in the basic technique of your stroke which will show up when you have to move rapidly to make the stroke.

In the next part of the book you will find details of how I recommend the strokes should be executed; but the execution is only what I call the middle part of a stroke, and I always try to impress upon my students that the preparation for the stroke and the recovery from the stroke are every bit as important. If you think about it no one can be expected to make the perfect stroke if he has not arrived at the right place in relation to the shuttle, and to be in the right place requires the proper preparation. By the same token a player may execute a beautiful stroke, but if he is flat on his back after he has hit the shuttle, the whole thing was a waste of time, and that is what I mean by 'recovery'.

THE GRIP

Where should we start with these basic techniques then? I think the holding of the racket is as good a place as any.

Shake hands with a friend: a normal, firm handshake without trying to crush his fingers. That is how you should hold a badminton racket to play strokes on the right-hand side of your body. Take hold of your racket, have a look at Fig. 1

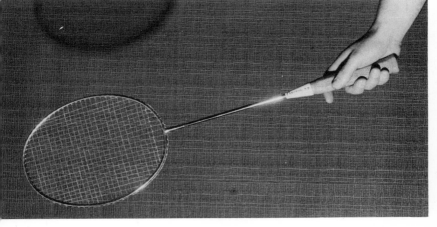

Fig. 1. The Forehand Grip.

and let us run through the check points. Is the 'V' formed by the thumb and index finger on the top edge of the racket handle? Are the fingers slightly spread along the handle and NOT bunched together like a fist? Is the index finger higher up the handle than the thumb? If your grip checks out on all these points then you have an orthodox *forehand grip*. This should be a firm but relaxed grip: there must be no feeling of tension in the wrist. You should feel that you can control the racket mainly with the thumb, index finger and little finger, which means that you have to get the racket out of the palm of your hand and into the fingers. This is of paramount importance.

I mentioned that there must be no feeling of tension in the wrist. If your wrist does feel stiff, it probably means that you are holding the racket too tightly, a very common fault with the beginner, and a fault which must be overcome as soon as possible. Try this little test. Take the racket in the forehand grip and grip it very tightly, the face of the racket should be vertical to the floor. Now, move the racket rapidly up and down as if you were trying to drive a nail into the floor with the edge of the racket. You should hear a swishing noise. Now do exactly the same again, but this time hold the racket as loosely as possible, the only firm pressure being with the thumb and index finger. I am sure you will hear a much louder swishing noise. This is no gimmick. It is highly significant, for the increased swish you get means that the head of the racket is travelling much faster. Later on when you practise smashes and clears, it is this speed in the head of the racket that you will be trying to develop. A relaxed hold on the racket is the first step to achieving it. Don't be afraid that the racket will fly from your hand. It very rarely does. You will find, with experience, that no matter how loosely you hold the racket, when the head swings through to the point of impact the grip automatically tightens without your thinking about it.

This, then, is the forehand grip which is used by most people for shots played on the forehand side of the body. A great many players find that this is also an all-purpose grip which they can use to play shots on the left-hand side of the body as well, i.e. the backhand. What I would advise you to do now is to play as much as you can and think about the way you hold your racket while playing. I know this is not always easy in the heat of a game, but try to concentrate particularly on that firm but still relaxed grip. If you are very lucky, you may become one of those fortunate players who can cope with all sorts of shots using the same grip, but it is more likely that you will find that it is easier to change the grip slightly to play shots on the backhand wing.

Take hold of the racket in the forehand grip, hold it out in front of you face vertical to the floor, and now turn the racket head a quarter of a turn to the outside of your body. Have a look at Fig. 2. Your thumb should now be resting

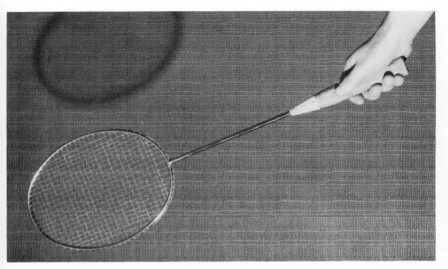

Fig. 2. The Backhand Grip.

on the flat side of the handle of the racket and it should be higher up the handle than the index finger. Press hard with the thumb and you will feel the tremendous amount of leverage you can now exert against the handle and therefore against the backhand face of the racket. It is this leverage that will provide the power you will need for some of the backhand shots we shall discuss later.

There is a third grip frequently used in badminton which I have left until last, not because it is unimportant, but because I would like you to master the orthodox forehand and backhand grips first. This other grip is illustrated in Fig. 3

Fig. 3. The 'Frying-pan' or 'Pan-handle' Grip (by a
left-handed player in this case).

and is usually referred to as the 'frying-pan' grip. This grip
is achieved by turning the racket from the forehand grip
through 90 degrees so that the face of the racket is hori-
zontal to the floor, like the palm of the hand, and the 'V'
of the thumb and index finger runs down the back, flat
edge of the handle.

The main advantages of this grip are that as the face of the
racket is always square to the net, no change in grip is needed
to play shots on the forehand and the backhand, provided
you are hitting a shuttle still above the tape. More important,

the 'frying-pan' grip enables players to execute very sharp dabbing shots at the net and consequently it is frequently employed by the lady in a mixed doubles game. However, as this grip tends to lock the wrist, and thereby causes lack of power, it is not advisable to use it for the power strokes deeper back in court.

So much for the 'frying-pan'. I want you to know that it is there and that it has a valuable use, but for the time being I would prefer you to work really hard on the orthodox backhand and forehand grips until you become quite fluent in changing from one to the other. Whenever you have a racket in your hand, try twirling it around and arriving at a selected grip. If you can, have a rally with a partner and push the shuttle rapidly back and forth to each side of the body, using the proper grip for each stroke. Work at it until your movements become automatic.

THE WRIST ACTION

All that I have said about grips and holding the racket has been leading up to the outstanding feature of stroke play in badminton, the wrist action. It is the wrist that governs most of the art of deception, an art which must be mastered by all who wish to reach the top in this game. It is the action of the wrist which imparts speed to the head of the racket—that in one shot produces the powerful snap that can make the shuttle leave the racket at over 100 m.p.h. but in another, when it is checked, can send the shuttle gently floating over the net. I have already shown you one way to achieve speedy wrist action: the almost loose grip of the racket, *in the fingers*. The other vitally important technique is known as 'cocking' the wrist. This means that for forehand shots the wrist must be cocked back as far as possible. See Fig. 4. You will find that you cannot do this unless you have a relaxed grip.

Try this on your shots played overhead on the forehand.

Try to get the wrist fully cocked at the end of your back-swing, then, as the arm comes forward, the wrist should whip the racket head forward to meet the shuttle. I shall deal

Fig. 4. 'Cocking' the Wrist.

much more fully with this aspect when I discuss the strokes, but just for the time being I want you to experiment and see how much you can bring the wrist into your game. As you will discover later the amount of wrist cocking will vary according to the power you wish to put into the shot, but a certain amount of cocking is needed even on the most delicate 'touch' shots—and remember, the wrist must be cocked back for ALL shots. On backhand strokes exactly the same principle applies except, of course, that the wrist is cocked in the opposite direction. In both cases the wrist must lead INTO the shot. When you have time to spare and you can't get on court, providing you have a wall to hand, try this practice. I recommend it for all standards of player and still use it myself today. Just take a battered shuttle and play a rally with yourself by hitting the shuttle against the wall. Use a snappy wristy action only and, after a time, you will be surprised at the force you can use. The shuttle will fly back at you in all directions, but this is the idea, and it will teach you to manœuvre your racket very rapidly from one side to the other.

FOOTWORK

If you can master the above you will have gone a long way to becoming a dexterous stroke player, but no matter how adroit you may become at handling a racket, as you may already have discovered, you still cannot produce a good stroke unless your body is in the right place in relation to the shuttle. What puts your body into the right position is your feet. Hence, footwork is a subject that should be studied by players at all levels. Footwork is the most common weakness in badminton players above the novice stage and I have demonstrated this point many times in practice sessions. So many players are able to execute an almost perfect stroke, whilst they are stationary and providing the shuttle is fed to them in exactly the right place. But, break down this perfect situation and make the player run to hit the shuttle and you will find that now he is sadly lacking. Good footwork will enable you to get to the shuttle in time to balance; then you can concentrate on playing the accurate shot. Bad footwork will mean scrambling to reach the shuttle, which will result in a hurried and therefore imperfectly timed stroke. Test yourself; if you find you can usually reach the shuttle to play the shot you want to, as hard as you want to, that it goes where it ought to go and that you can *immediately* move to another position in court, there is nothing wrong with your footwork. If this does not happen to you, then your footwork could be improved. But don't worry, your footwork can be improved.

There is no mystique about footwork, for what we really mean by it is court-covering, movement, a means of travelling from one part of the court to another as simply and economically as possible, but quickly. Please try to remember that, ideally, we want to get behind the shuttle so that we can play the shot moving IN to it. This means that we must move fast enough to intercept the shuttle in the most advantageous position for us. Further, just prior to actually making the stroke, a moment of stillness, of balance, is desirable. This enables the feet to be properly aligned and the body weight correctly distributed for the shot to be played.

Imagine the situation in which you have just put the shuttle into your opponent's half of the court and he is just about to make his stroke. This is the danger-point for any player, but for the beginner, who has not enough experience to know what can be done with the shuttle, it is even worse. At this time the novice will usually stand flat footed waiting to see where the shuttle is played and only when the shuttle is half-way home will he be able to move to reply. As his knowledge of the game increases so the player will be able to eliminate certain possibilities, and as his experience grows he will learn to look for signs that will indicate what is the most likely shot to be played. With confident anticipation, the advanced player will already have decided, before the shuttle is struck, where he thinks it is going and will have shifted his balance in that direction.

The situation described above is one of the rare moments when no movement is taking place on your part, but it won't last long. So be ready to move away, at speed, the moment you receive the signal. To do so a good position of readiness from which you can move with ease in any direction is essential. Face the net, feet about shoulder width apart, knees slightly bent (this latter point I think is very important as so many people tend to stand with knees braced, which undoub-

Fig. 5. Position of Readiness.

tedly impedes a fast getaway). Get on to the balls of your feet so that your weight is slightly forward. Do not allow your feet to become glued to the floor, keep them fidgeting around whilst you wait for your opponent's reply. Hold the racket, with a bent arm, slightly in front of you, and above all, KEEP THE RACKET HEAD UP. See Fig. 5.

Please try to adopt this position of readiness at all times

when you are not actually involved in playing or moving to play the shuttle. It is so important because it really will help to give you an edge when you have to move quickly. From this basic position you are in the best stance to move off in any direction. This is where footwork comes in. If you are able to play badminton, you are able to run and so I don't have to teach you that. What I would now suggest is that you find out for yourself how you can best get from point 'A' to point 'B'.

Many theories have been expounded on the best footwork for moving about a badminton court, but I always maintain that the movement which comes most naturally to the players must be the best. When I am coaching a player I normally find out what footwork is most natural to him and then try to improve what he has got, rather than try to enforce any pet ideas of mine on him. As I cannot be there and observe you, what you must do is attempt to examine how you yourself move about the court. First of all observe how other people move, then think about your own footwork. Get a friend to help you in this when you are playing in a game as it is more difficult to move naturally when concentrating on how you are moving.

You will find that footwork can be classified under two broad headings. Firstly, the chassé—a shuffling action where one foot takes a step and the other foot is brought up to it, but does not pass it. Secondly, running—the natural action we all adopt when we want to move rapidly from one spot to another. So saying, it would seem logical that to run naturally would be the best means of rapidly covering a badminton court. In a great many cases this is so, but there are advantages in chasséing as well.

Remember what we have actually discussed. Firstly, the idea is to arrive at a certain position in order to deliver a particular stroke, on balance and momentarily still before commencing the stroke. Are you able to do that? If not, it means that either your footwork is slow or that you have moved too late to intercept the shuttle, probably because you waited until the shuttle had travelled into your court before you started to move. No matter how fleet of foot you may be you still won't give yourself a fair chance if you delay making your move until the shuttle has almost reached its destination.

Secondly, and this is just as important; when you arrive at the point where you are going to make the stroke, are your feet correctly positioned? Have your friend take a look at this too. I deal more fully with the feet position in the Strokes Section but, broadly speaking, these general rules apply. For forehand shots the left shoulder points to the net and the feet are comfortably apart at roughly 45 degrees to the net with the left foot nearer to the side line than the right. For backhand shots the position is reversed with the right foot ahead of and nearer to the side line than the left. You will have to go more deeply into the stroke before you work out the exact positioning of the feet to suit you, but the general principle of left foot leads on a forehand and right foot leads on a backhand, applies. I suggest you try playing a few imaginary shots—you can do this in your garden—on the forehand and backhand and check that your grip, stance and balance are correct for the circumstances. Then play a rally with your friend, slowly at first and then build up speed, just concentrating on this feature of positioning and footwork.

So you see, you now have the dual problem that not only must you have movement but the movement must be such that you arrive at your destination in a given manner. And that is what footwork is all about.

Undoubtedly, straightforward running is the fastest means of covering any distance but the danger is that you could overrun and find yourself striking at the shuttle as you pass by. That is why I said that the chassé had its advantages. This method, particularly when moving backwards to take a shot overhead on the forehand, ensures that the feet are always correctly placed to play the shot. Likewise, I think chasséing is best for moving sideways—as you will have to a great deal in mixed doubles. Have a go at this; you will find it strange at first, but if you get on your toes and try to skip lightly across the court, it will come. However, when you practise it, do be sure to arrive in the correct striking stance for backhand or forehand shots.

To move forward at speed, I would always recommend the run. Most people are happier moving forwards and find less trouble adjusting their feet correctly for the stroke they are to play. I must mention one peculiarity when moving forwards to deal with a low return in the forecourt; to play this shot I usually advise that the right foot leads. Now this contradicts the general principles of forehand footwork but nevertheless, you will find that with the right foot forward you have a longer reach and a better balance.

To play a high backhand shot you may prefer to chassé, but as a general rule, you should find that to turn your back to the net and run will be more effective.

Another method of moving which has found favour and success with some players, mainly in the singles game, is what I can only call 'taking steps'. Here, the player calculates the number of strides he needs to take him from one position to another given position, to arrive in exactly the right stance to play the stroke. It is argued in favour of this method that once a player has made his calculation and practised sufficiently it becomes a reflex action to ensure his being always in the right striking position with the minimum effort, without even having to adjust the feet. I would suggest, however, that you gain more experience of the shuttle's behaviour and concentrate on the basic points I mentioned before you try 'taking steps'.

There you are then. Perhaps you will now think that chasing after a shuttle can be a little more scientific than you first thought. But for heaven's sake, please don't worry about it. Footwork is not something to be mastered as a technique in itself: it must be grafted on to your game. So start grafting. Take it in easy stages by consciously thinking about your movements, and get a friend to help you. Experiment with the different methods I have described both by selecting a particular manœuvre and by trying different ways of achieving the same objective. Play a game of shadow badminton. That is, when you are by yourself plan out sequences of rallies such as you would expect to encounter in a game and carry out the most effective footwork to enable you to get into position to play the correct stroke and move off again quickly.

Just a couple of final tips. If you are a tall player take short steps. Whatever you decide, short initial steps will give you a quicker start. Make the last step you take the longest. There are going to be occasions, during fast rallies, when all your careful footwork will be forgotten. This happens to everyone and you will just have to sort your feet out as best you can. Do not be dogmatic about the position of your feet. Even the best players frequently find they have miscalculated and another skip, hop or slither is necessary to make an adjustment. You are not a ballet dancer, it is your effectiveness that counts.

Part Three: THE STROKES

This section of the book is devoted to the strokes used in badminton and is set out so that you may refer to each stroke as required. The intention is that you should take from it what you need when you find a particular stroke repeatedly ineffective. It is not intended that you should slavishly follow everything I say in an attempt to become a carbon copy of my perfect stroke player. That is neither necessary nor desirable.

What you should be doing at this stage in your development is finding out what sort of strokes you have to play in order to win a game. After all, to win is the object of the exercise! Of course, such knowledge will only come through the experience of playing games and so, for the moment, this should be your primary task. Every time you play you must ask yourself, 'What kind of stroke won/lost me that point?' Find the most effective means of winning a rally rather than worry too much about whether your feet are in the right place or whether your arm is bent, etc.

I maintain that each one of us is an individual and we each have our own unique way of doing things. I may play a stroke quite differently to you but that does not mean that I am right and you are wrong. The criterion must be 'Which way produces the best result?' *When* and *where* you make your shots and the *effect* they have on the game is more important than *how* you make them.

However, there is, in most cases, a better way of executing a stroke, and my suggestions are based, quite apart from my own observations, upon the experience and experiments of very many really great players over the years. If you develop an unorthodox stroke, it may well get you by in a poor class of badminton but it may break down in a hard game, *where you are pressed.* So you must not be too ready to think your unorthodox stroke is all right. In addition, of course, scientific principles will dictate whether one method of doing something is mechanically more efficient than another. Eventually you will have to strike a balance between your individuality and how I suggest you do the stroke in order to find the most effective means *for you.* But do try my suggestions as soon as possible. Do not allow yourself to develop a faulty, ineffective technique as this will be difficult to rectify later on.

A final note of warning. So many beginners, in their eagerness to get the stroke right, try to concentrate on several points at once. This is nearly impossible, so please don't try. Most of the points you need to remember must be done subconsciously. So take it easy. Concentrate on just one point at a time.

THE SERVICE

Of all the strokes, the service—possibly the most important stroke of the lot—presents the greatest opportunity to express one's own personality and style. For, especially with the low service, it is true to say that it doesn't matter how you do it *as long as it is effective.*

What are you going to do about making yours effective then? I suggest that you start in the simplest way possible. Stand near the centre service line, two to three feet behind the short service line, with the left foot leading. Hold the shuttle in the left hand—I suggest that you hold it by the tips of the feathers so that it drops plumb, slightly ahead of the body, and just allow it to drop. As you release the shuttle, swing the racket (held in the forehand grip) gently forwards to meet it and hit the shuttle diagonally across the net to fall just over the short service line into your opponent's service court. That is the *short* or *low* service, which I imagine is very much like the service you have been doing up to now.

If the player receiving your service is one of those people who allows the shuttle to fall until it is almost on the floor before he attempts to strike it, then it follows that it doesn't matter how good, bad or indifferent your service may be. He can do nothing with it apart from lift it in the air. On the other hand, if your opponent is one of those fierce fellows who is able to rush forward and drive the shuttle straight back into your chest, it means that the service is not effective and needs to be improved. This is where long, arduous practice is needed, for you will have to find the best style of serving for you to produce the most effective result.

The best players in the world experimented with many different styles of serving in their badminton careers before discovering the particular style that suited them best, and this is what you must do. You can often practise serving just by yourself, although it is obviously better if a friend can stand at the other side of the net to help you. Undoubtedly the best way to improve your service is to try out the different methods whilst you are actually playing in a game. When an opponent is trying to beat you, there will be no doubt whether or not your service is effective.

I would now like you to think about the many different things you can do in serving, but please, please remember my earlier warning to concentrate on just one thing at a time. Do not become impatient and discard an idea if it does not work first time. A good service will take a long time to perfect, and, before you start your practice in earnest, I suggest that you read up the Laws of serving and make sure you fully understand them.

Though there are many and varied styles of serving, as I

have said, there are common factors present in all of them. It is vital that you get the fundamentals right before you add your own flair. Your aim is to direct the shuttle into your opponent's court so that it just skims the top of the net, and to do this requires a great deal of precision.

The first basic you have to consider is your grip. This must be comfortable and allow you to exercise the control necessary to obtain precision. In the simple service you did the grip was the orthodox forehand grip which if it suits you is fine, but you might find that you can control the head of the racket better if you shorten the grip by holding it slightly higher up the handle. If you do try this it is important to get back to the normal grip immediately after hitting the serve.

The next thing to remember is the stance. This must also be comfortable and relaxed. Stand tall, don't crouch. You will probably lead with your left foot but if you prefer to have the right foot nearer to the net, this is quite in order, particularly if you find that you can move faster after you have hit the shuttle. In either event, at the start of the service, your weight should be slightly over your back foot.

Now for the arm movement. For the short service, little power is required, and therefore a strong arm movement is not necessary. In this shot, the shuttle is guided, almost pushed over the net, rather than hit. If you find that the main fault with your short service is that the shuttle is passing too high over the net, you can be fairly certain that there is too much movement in the head of the racket and that you are hitting at the shuttle rather than stroking it forwards.

In all strokes in badminton the action of the wrist plays a very prominent part, *with the exception of this one stroke*. For the short service it is desirable that the wrist is held very firm in a cocked back position. This will keep the head of the racket in the same plane and prevent it from wobbling about, so providing greater control when you stroke the shuttle. There must also be some sort of backswing to the racket. You will see some players take theirs right back,

Fig. 6. A typical lady's short service with a restricted action.
(a) Preliminary stance—firm wrist, cocked back.
(b) Impact. Arm pivots from shoulder. Racket head 'pushes' shuttle. Server on toes, leaning forward.
(c) Follow-through. Moving forward into net with racket up.

whilst others hardly seem to move the racket at all and just 'pop' the shuttle over the net. Be that as it may, once you have found the sort of swing that suits you this must be 'grooved' into you to ensure absolute consistency in serving.

As your arm comes forward to meet the shuttle with the racket head, so the weight of the body is shifted from the back foot until it is slightly over the front foot. Take care not to walk into the service—this is illegal. As you make contact with the shuttle you will find it helpful if you rise well up onto your toes; even to the point of nearly overbalancing. This could be very important for, as you will learn later, it is essential that immediately you have delivered the service you are able to move forward to deal with any possible net return. See Fig. 6.

These are the basic ingredients and if I were you I would concentrate on them for the time being. Think about incorporating your own style, not for the sake of style, but with the idea of producing a more effective service. In a later section I shall have a little more to say on the subject.

The Flick Service

The flick service is intended to deceive the opponent and therefore, in its initial approach, it must exactly resemble your normal short service. The idea is that you will lead an aggressive opponent into believing that you are going to do your normal short service and then, at the last moment, with a powerful flick of the wrist the shuttle will be popped over his head, just out of reach of his outstretched racket, to land near the long service line for doubles. This is an extremely valuable service to have, if used sparingly against those opponents who like to rush the service. It fails dismally if it lacks deception and the deception is created mainly by the wrist action. This is why I suggested that your short service commenced with the wrist cocked back. By so doing not only can you develop an accurate short service but the wrist is now in the best position for imparting the strong flick required. The other essential ingredient of the flick service is the follow through. In the short service the follow through was a very easy action but in the flick the racket head will need to be lifted much higher and more sharply. It is also important that the forearm and shoulder should follow through with the action. If you try this service just by wrist action alone you will find that you are snatching at the shuttle, and the whole effect will be destroyed.

This service will need a lot of practice to be effective and if you find that the opposition has no trouble in dealing with it you can be sure that it either lacks deception, or the receiver is standing too deep in court.

The High Service

The action for the high service is just like the basic low service I outlined previously, except that everything about it is stronger. There is no deception in this service. The intention is to send the shuttle to a considerable height to land either on the long service line in the doubles game or on the back boundary line in singles. Therefore, in view of the power needed for this shot, take a firmer stance with the feet slightly wider apart and, this time, I think you would do better with the left foot leading. Take a much longer backswing and, as you do so, shift your weight more on to your back foot. Your arm should come back farther and your wrist should be cocked back even more. Start the forward swing with more speed and, as the hand comes opposite the shuttle, allow the wrist to whip the racket head through with all its power. Make no attempt to check the racket, but let it follow through for a while in the direction you want the shuttle to take, and then let it swing through quite naturally up in the air and towards the left shoulder. See Fig. 7. As you swing, your weight will fall on to your leading foot and the power you you put into the shot should drag you up on to your toes. At first you will probably be inclined to snatch at the shuttle and mis-time the stroke, so be particularly careful to keep your head down until you have hit the shuttle. Don't be too anxious to see where it is going, but do watch the shuttle

Fig. 7. The High Service.
(a) Preliminary Stance. Good backswing and plenty of room for the shuttle to drop.
(b) Follow-through. Quite freely and naturally over the left shoulder.

right on to the racket face until impact. The strong wrist action will give height to the shuttle but the straight arm on impact will give the distance. This is quite a natural stroke, so let it be natural and give it all you've got.

The Drive Service

As its name implies, this is a service in which the shuttle is struck very hard on a flat path and sent to the back of the opponent's court—usually to his backhand corner. Against players who leave a big gap in this corner or those who have a definite weakness in defending their backhand, the service can be of value. However, it must be appreciated that the shot can boomerang against you for, due to its speed, it only needs the opponent to get his racket in the way and the shuttle can be put very quickly back into your own court.

I don't think I would bother too much with the drive service if I were you. Your time can be far better employed on perfecting the other types of service. Another objection I have to inexperienced players trying the drive service is the ease with which it is possible to contravene the Laws governing service. In an attempt to get the path of the shuttle really flat a player will often strike the shuttle above his waist or allow a part of the head of his racket to be above some part of his hand. Both are very bad faults, all too frequently committed by experienced players who should know better.

It is only with the service that the player has absolute choice as to where the shuttle will be when he wants to hit it, how he will stand in order to hit it and how long he will take over making his stroke. For the service is the only occasion when the shuttle is not moving prior to the stroke being made. In all the other strokes in badminton the player will have to make some movement in order to intercept the shuttle in its flight, often at speed, and he will have to make his stroke in such a manner that he can move to another part of his court immediately afterwards. It is therefore most important that you fully appreciate that there are really three parts to all the strokes I am now going to deal with:

1. The initial preparation—by this I mean arriving in the most advantageous position to play the stroke with the feet correctly placed and on balance.
2. The Stroke—the action of making the shot.
3. Recovery—that is recovery of balance and movement to the next most suitable position.

In my opinion, 1 and 3 can often be more important than 2—a technically perfect stroke. This we discussed in the previous part, so I am going to assume that you now fully appreciate the importance of these two factors in your play and I shall now concentrate on the middle bit, the actual technique of the stroke.

RETURN OF SERVICE

The foremost idea in your mind, when receiving service, should be to hit the shuttle down. The where and when I shall cover in the next section. At the moment, I only want you to consider HOW.

The stance you adopt should be the same no matter whether you are playing singles or doubles. You have to be capable of dealing with every type of service. Stand in your receiving court, about 3 feet from the centre service line and one to two feet behind the short service line (ladies may be happier about 3 feet back). Place your left foot forward so that your feet are comfortably apart and you are evenly balanced. Bend the knees a little and lean slightly forward, so that your weight is mainly over your front foot. Hold your racket in front of you, with the head of the racket up and just above the height of the net, in a forehand grip. See Figs. 8 and 9.

Fig. 8. A right-handed player receiving service from the left court. A good position, but as his confidence grows he will be able to 'toe the line'.

Experiment with this stance until you are quite sure that you are comfortable and able to move at speed, equally well, both forwards and backwards. Ultimately you will find that the nearer to the short service line you can stand the more effective you can be in dealing with a short service. However,

Fig. 9. A left-handed player from the right court. An alert, aggressive position and you would not expect a lady to stand much nearer to the short service line than this.

it will take time to develop the ability to stand so close, and still be able to get back to deal with the flick service.

Your reply to a short serve will depend on how early you can intercept the shuttle. In all cases, once you have defined it as a short service, push off with the back foot, with the racket raised in front of you, towards the shuttle. Do not wait until it reaches you, but cut it off as soon as it crosses the net. The number of steps you will have to take will depend on your starting position in court, but it does not matter which foot you land on to play the shot. If you can meet the shuttle just as it crosses, and is still above the net (not before!) a sharp dab downwards is the answer. You will not have time for a backswing so you will have to rely on a wristy action for power.

When a downward stroke is not possible, you will have to drop the racket head beneath the shuttle and stroke it back, as close to the tape as possible, just as you would do with any net return. If the shuttle has dropped well below the height of the tape you are faced with the same alternatives as we discuss in net play (page 66): either a cross-court net shot or an underarm clear to the back. In the former case make sure the opposition is not standing there, and if you clear make sure it is high and deep, preferably to the backhand.

If a HIGH service is delivered, you will have ample time to move back, to deal with the shot as you would any other overhead stroke. In doubles, your best reply is a smash.

You may be deceived by a FLICK service and if you really are deceived you must make the best of it. Move quickly backwards and, if you can, smash the shuttle. Often you will not be able to get behind a good flick service and you will be left with either a drop shot or a clear. This is what your opposition have hoped for and so you must ensure that your reply is to a spot they have left unguarded.

Because a DRIVE service is so flat and fast the best answer is simply to put the face of your racket in its path. Sometimes it will be sufficient to allow the shuttle to bounce off it. But if you are able to use your wrist, you could flick it downwards or upwards to a suitable space.

THE OVERHEAD FOREHAND STROKES

The SMASH is the main point-winning stroke where the shuttle is hit sharply downwards into the opponent's court.

The CLEAR is usually defensive in that here the intention is to strike the shuttle into the air, from the back of your own court to the base line of your opponent's court.

The DROP SHOT, as its name implies, is a shot played from the back of your own court into the forecourt of your opponent. The shot can either be the SLOW, falling almost perpendicularly just over the net, or the FAST, which arrives at its destination more quickly but lands a little deeper in the opposing forecourt area.

I want you to consider these three strokes together as in the interest of deception the initial action for them must appear identical.

Forget your racket for the moment and just throw an imaginary ball as far and as high as you can. If your action resembles a dart thrower down at the local, then it isn't very good for our purpose. But if it is like a first-class cricketer throwing a ball from the boundary, we are half-way to making a good overhead, forehand stroke. Try it a few times and then take up your racket and try exactly the same action again. Let us have a look at what you should be doing in greater detail.

Start with the feet; they should be comfortably apart, shoulder width should be about right, in the fore and aft position I described earlier for forehand strokes. You must be in a sideways-on position, with the left shoulder pointing towards the net. Swing the racket back, underarm, and as you do this you will find that your wrist quite naturally turns away from the body: cock the wrist back. Bend the arm at the elbow so that your hand is behind your head and the racket is allowed to drop down behind your back, still keeping your wrist cocked. (You will only be able to achieve this if you have that relaxed grip.) Whilst you are getting into this

Fig. 10. The Overhead Forehand Strokes.
(a) Completion of Backswing. Notice: feet in fore and aft position, body sideways to the net. Left hand pointing at shuttle. Racket in backscratching position. Weight over back foot.

'back-scratching' position your weight should be shifting on to your back foot and as it does so your left foot will start to creep forwards. At this point you will find it helpful to point your left hand at the shuttle. This will not only help your balance but will also assist in 'sighting' the shuttle. See Fig. 10a.

(b) Just before Impact. Arm straightening—BUT wrist still cocked.
(c) Point of Impact. Shoulders are now turning and body weight is
    transferring on to leading foot.

(d) Follow-through. After a smash, full swing of racket naturally to the left. Weight now entirely on leading foot.

(e) Just after Impact on a Clear. Shoulders turning, weight over leading foot, but follow-through will not be so vigorous.

You are now ready to start the throwing action and your weight should be entirely on your back foot. The leading foot will only barely touch the floor to maintain balance. You can now throw the head of the racket at the shuttle and follow through as you practised earlier.

Practise what we have done so far by concentrating on getting the feet right, the shoulder pointing to the net, a nice easy movement that brings your racket into the back-scratching position and then into the full throwing action. When you feel quite confident about this you can move on to consider the next stages.

In all the overhead strokes your body, arm and wrist co-ordinate to put maximum power into the stroke. As your racket head swings forward to meet the shuttle your weight is transferred completely from the back foot to the front foot and so all your weight is going forward. The elbow leads the action and you should straighten your arm sharply as you throw the racket head upwards, but with the wrist still cocked back. (Fig. 10b). The wrist must be smartly uncocked only on impact so that, if your timing is accurate, the elbow and wrist straighten the arm and racket just as you hit the shuttle.

In the SMASH you are going to hit very steeply down-wards and to do so you must get 'on top' of the shuttle as it were. Your arm must still be straight at the point of impact (Fig. 10c). Your racket should meet the shuttle at a spot approximately over the leading shoulder and, because of the force used, your follow through will be very vigorous. Let the racket head follow the direction of the shuttle for a time then keep swinging down in a natural manner, *past the left side of the body*. See Fig. 10d. As you follow through, your right foot will come forward, ahead of the left foot, to maintain bal-ance.

With the CLEAR, because the intention is to hit the shuttle high and deep, an upward trajectory is necessary, and to achieve this the shuttle should be struck slightly behind

the point for the smash, roughly over the right sh
The follow through will not carry so far as in the
because you are hitting upwards, but in other respects it is
the same. See Fig. 10e.

In the FAST DROP SHOT the shuttle is contacted in
the same position as for the smash and in the SLOW
DROP SHOT the loopy trajectory described by the shuttle
is achieved by slowing down the racket movement just before
impact and by not allowing the wrist to uncock quite so
quickly. The follow through for the fast drop shot will
closely resemble that of the smash, while for the slow drop
shot you should just let it take its normal course. Remember
drop shots are intended to deceive and so it is not sufficient
just to execute the stroke; you must look as though you are
going to do one of the powerful ones instead!

There are an awful lot of points to remember and I am
quite sure that you will manage most of them quite comfortably, but if you find that your stroke is not effective think
about all these points I have mentioned, in turn. Try to
select just one which you think may be at the root of the
trouble and concentrate on that for a while. Here again, a
friend may be able to spot something wrong that you hadn't
noticed. Take only one point at a time and do not try to
cope with them all at once.

THE OVERHEAD BACKHAND STROKES

Just as I dealt with the smash, clear and drop shot on the
forehand together, so I am going to deal with these strokes
on the backhand. Without doubt, the clear is the most
important in this group. Most players, and especially
novices, find the ·backhand corner of the court rather
difficult to cope with and naturally their opponents tend to
take advantage of this fact. A sound *backhand clear* has therefore come to be recognised as the main defensive measure
to be taken. As you will learn later, I think it is very bad to

assume that a shot played high to this area *must* be taken on
the backhand but, at the same time, I do think that the
complete player should be able to play these strokes. Quite
apart from which you will probably have seen one of the
'greats' playing a full length backhand clear, making it look
as easy as falling off a log, and you will want to do the same.

In my opinion the ability to execute an effective, easy
backhand clear depends almost entirely on a very powerful
wrist-flicking action and perfect timing. These two factors
are sufficient, but one without the other will not do. Now, not
all of us are gifted with super-strong wrists, but that does not
mean that we cannot do this stroke. If our wrist will not give
us the necessary power we must compensate by making
better use of the other parts of the body in connection with
the shot.

I am now going to outline how I recommend you should
start to practise the backhand clear. It won't work at first,
but don't worry. Get a friend to see if he can spot where you
are going wrong and then, just as you did with the forehand
strokes, take one point at a time and work on it.

Stand facing the left sideline so that your right shoulder
is pointing to the net. Place your feet sideways to the net, with
the right foot nearer to the sideline. In other words, it is
almost exactly the reverse position to the forehand footwork.
Using your backhand grip, drop the racket head over your
left shoulder to the back-scratching position and as you do so
ensure that your elbow is pointing upwards towards the
oncoming shuttle. At the same time swivel the hips to the
left so that your back is exposed to the net. Your knees
should be very slightly bent, with all your weight on the left
foot. So, in this position. you should feel that your whole
body, from the feet, through the hips and shoulders, right
up to your wrist, is coiled up like a spring waiting to be
released. Your aim will be to contact the shuttle immediately
above the right shoulder and as you see the shuttle approach-
ing this spot, whip the racket head upwards to meet it—

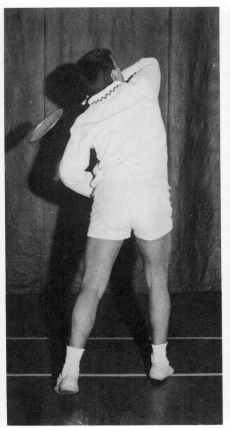

Fig. 11. Overhead Backhand.
(a) Stance just prior to hitting. Back turned to net. Elbow pointing up.
(b) Point of Impact—with a straight arm.
Note: The position of Peter's feet differs from the description in the text in that now his right foot is behind the left. In other words, as he prepares for the shot his weight is over his RIGHT foot and transfers to his LEFT foot as he makes the stroke. Some players find this footwork easier for this shot, particularly if the shuttle has passed them. However, as the opposition cannot be seen at the time the shuttle is struck, I suggest you try the other method first.

with a straight arm. Your elbow leads the movement, pointing at the shuttle, followed by the forearm with the wrist still cocked. As the arm straightens out to make impact, snap the racket head at and through the shuttle; flick at the shuttle, but in an upward direction, NOT outwards. For the moment forget about distance; just concentrate on height and the length will come quite naturally later.

While you are busy with this arm and wrist action you will probably have forgotten the rest of your body. Never mind, you can only do one thing at a time. You will almost certainly find that the shot is not going quite right and so, once you feel more accustomed to the arm action, try to let the body help you. When you were in the back-scratching position, all your weight was on your left foot. The throwing action you are going to make is a violent one and so, as you throw the racket upwards, all your weight will shift on to the right foot. As you do this and make the arm movement, twist your hips to the right so that your make contact with the shuttle with the right shoulder pointing to the net, *but keep your feet in the same position*. The follow through is negligible as the elbow will lock your straight arm at impact. See Fig. 11.

If you are able to co-ordinate all these movements and time the final hitting action, a very powerful shot should result. However, it does take a lot of practice to get the timing just right, so keep at it and I am sure your efforts will be rewarded in due course.

While you are practising this backhand clear, which, until it is effective, will not get you out of trouble, you will still find in the course of a game that the shuttle is coming to your backhand corner and you will have to do something about it. Normally I do not advise any delay in playing the shuttle for I believe you should be encouraged to meet the shuttle as early as possible. But I think the instance we are discussing could be an exception to the rule. If your clear is not effective when you try to play it overhead, try instead to let the shuttle fall to between shoulder and waist height and then using the same footwork, take a big swing at the shuttle, get underneath it and loft it to the back of the opponent's court. You will find that you need not drop the racket head behind your back although a long backswing is necessary. It is important that you strike the shuttle at arm's length, for if it is struck too near the body, the action will be cramped with ensuing loss of power. The follow through is also very important. You must let the racket head continue on its natural path without attempting to check it at all. To do so would mean snatching at the shuttle with, again, a loss of power. This particular 'swishing' stroke possibly requires more physical effort but less actual technique in the wrist action and timing. For this reason many of the continental ladies have adopted it as their standard clearance from the backhand. Don't be afraid, chaps, you won't be regarded as a cissy if you do it! Have a go at it but don't forget that although you will not point the elbow UPWARDS, it should still point AT the shuttle and the elbow leads the action as before with the wrist held back to give an upward snap as you hit the shuttle.

I do not wish to spend too much time on the backhand SMASH as you will have your time cut out working on the clear, and it is quite an ambitious shot. Very few of even the best players can claim to be really effective with the backhand smash unless it is a 'sitter' near the net. It is not a shot to be played from the base line area, nor even from as far back in court as you would expect to be able to play your forehand smash. But played from mid or forecourt area it can be very useful, if correctly placed.

The preliminary action for the smash is, as you would expect, identical to the clear, except that the wrist snaps the shuttle smartly downwards instead of upwards. As it is necessary to get on top of the shuttle to achieve this downward flick, it is better to contact the shuttle approximately 12 inches nearer to the net and nearer to the side line. This will allow a more pronounced follow through and the 'getting on top of the shuttle' effect.

DROP SHOTS on the backhand are again intended to deceive and so must be made to look just like the clear or smash in the preparation stage. Everything I have said about the forehand drop shots applies here as well. It is the slowing down of the action immediately prior to impact and the checking of the wrist that produces the SLOW drop shot. As for the FAST one, unless you can afford a considerable amount of practice there will probably be little distinction between the fast drop and the smash and so, for the time being, I think you would be well advised to treat the two as one, to be used as needs must. Reserve them until you have mastered the basic strokes.

THE DRIVES

Drives are a family of strokes where the shuttle has fallen too low to smash and yet you don't want to play a purely defensive stroke, that is, hit upwards. Ideally, you should hit the shuttle at about shoulder level but you will often play shots that have fallen below shoulder height—I don't mean off the floor!—and these are still drives. Your aim is to send the shuttle along a flat path as near parallel to the floor as possible and, no matter at what height you contact it, the shuttle should just skim the net.

Drives are mainly used by the man in mixed doubles but, of course, there is plenty of scope for their general use in the game, particularly when you want to rush the shuttle into your opponent's body or get it quickly past him. One of the great faults with players using this stroke is that so many feel it necessary to hit the shuttle as hard as possible. This is not the case, for though the drive is basically a fast stroke it offers a variety of placement shots as well.

Nevertheless I always advocate that at the start of the stroke you should allow a good backswing, very much on the lines of the overhead forehand shots. By doing this you are now not only able to call upon all the power you may need if you decide on a full-blooded drive but you can always cut down the pace should you wish.

Let us look at the forehand first. In the other strokes I have suggested the best footwork for you to use but, in this stroke, you have a choice. As it is a forehand shot, it would seem natural to adopt the normal forehand footwork with the left foot leading. However, a great many players feel that they can intercept the shuttle earlier and make a quicker recovery to the centre of the court if they play this shot off the 'wrong' foot, i.e. with the right foot leading. Try this method and see how you get on. Either way is right, and your decision will depend on which you find more effective. In both cases you must think of getting your body weight into the shot and this means that on the backswing your weight will be on the back foot and shift on to the front foot as you swing the racket forward. Don't worry too much about your footwork then, or at least, not for the moment. The time to start worrying is if you find it is the footwork that is letting you down. Your main aim is to ensure that you can meet the shuttle at the earliest possible moment, that you can control the direction of flight and that you can move quickly to play the next shot.

However you arrange your feet, your preliminary action with the racket will be very similar to the overhead clear. Get the racket well back and, by bending the elbow, and relaxing the wrist, allow the head of the racket to drop between the shoulder blades. In this position, the palm of your hand should be pointing UPWARDS, wrist cocked back. From here, throw the head of the racket at the shuttle, wrist leading, in an arc parallel to the floor. Your aim is to contact the shuttle as high as possible, at the full stretch of the arm, in front of and to the right of, the body. In other words, with drives, you are always thinking of moving *diagonally forwards* to meet the shuttle. As you make the shot, allow your body

Fig. 12. The Forehand Drive—off the 'wrong' foot, as executed by a master of this stroke, Tony Jordan.

to move into it, taking the weight on the leading foot. See Fig. 12.

Your wrist should only uncock as you strike the shuttle, and the degree to which you do uncock the wrist will help determine the path of the shuttle. You will find it helpful if you only partially uncock the wrist to send the shuttle straight down the line. To send it cross-court more snap will be required. In either event, hit firmly and try to hit 'through' the shuttle, keeping the face of the racket square to the shuttle's line of flight for as long as possible before allowing the racket to follow through across the body and in front of the left shoulder.

The backhand drive is exactly the reverse of the forehand except, of course, that the feet must be in the position outlined for the backhand clear. In fact for this drive, there could be some advantage in moving the right foot even more across towards the side line. A good backswing is needed again, bringing the racket hand opposite, if not touching, the left shoulder. The wrist is fully cocked back and, more important, the elbow points at the shuttle, *parallel to the ground*. At the start of the forward swing the face of the racket should be at right angles to the floor, so that the shuttle is contacted squarely. As before, fling the racket head at and through the shuttle. The elbow starts the action, then snaps the arm straight, and the wrist sharply uncocks just before impact, which takes place diagonally in front of the right foot. Follow through by keeping the racket square to the shuttle's line of flight for a time and then let it naturally swing round to the right. This will help to bring your body square to the net, and back to your position of readiness.

Earlier I mentioned that it was not always necessary to hit the shuttle as hard as possible. The PUSH is a variation of the drive and is played in exactly the same manner except that about 3 feet before you hit the shuttle you should slow down the action. Do not jerk it, just slow it down so that the shuttle is directed to a suitable spot in the opponent's forecourt. When you do this, your follow through will not be so pronounced, but keep a firm smooth action.

UNDERARM STROKES

These are strokes played from below net level because, for one reason or another, it was not possible to meet the shuttle earlier. Sometimes it will be difficult to tell the difference between an underarm shot and one of the rather low drives mentioned above, but such a fine distinction is not important.

As a defensive measure you may return the shuttle *high* with an underarm action either in reply to a smash, or when a drop shot has fallen to a low position close to the net. Deeper back in court, when the net does not present an obstruction, you will have a choice of playing the shuttle high, as before, or you could employ a low driving action to hit on a flatter plane.

As this latter action is so similar to the drives previously discussed I shall only add one thing. Be very careful how hard you hit the shuttle. If you hit the shuttle hard in an upward direction, your opponent has only to get his racket in the way and the shuttle will be back in your court before you can blink.

The shot we usually have in mind when we refer to underarm strokes is the underarm clear, or lob, as it is sometimes called. It is mainly used when the shuttle has to be played from well below the level of the net and in front of the short service line. (The nearer the shuttle is to the net, the more difficult it is to return—so practise your slow drop shot.)

Your intention with the underarm clear will be to hit the shuttle as high and as deep as you can, and the secret of this is to get well under the shuttle with the racket head. Usually, the shot will be played on the move and so your footwork is important.

On the forehand I am sure you will do better if you play the shot off the 'wrong' foot, i.e. with the right foot leading. The last step you take should be a long one, a lunge if you like. As you make the lunge, the arm action will be very like the action for the high service. That is, as you move forwards, commence the backswing until your right hand is opposite your right shoulder, elbow pointing down, wrist cocked back. You should contact the shuttle in front of and a little to the right of your leading foot. Swing your arm downwards and forwards so that it straightens on impact and your wrist whips under and through the shuttle. Follow through upwards and to your left (do not hit the net—this is a fault).

On the backhand, as usual, the procedure is reversed. Backhand footwork again, but lunge the right foot into a wider stance. You will usually approach the shot in a hurry and throwing your weight on to the leading foot will help you to get underneath the shuttle. But, if the step is too wide and you lose balance, you will have great difficulty in moving away. After the backswing, which should bring your right hand opposite your left shoulder, your elbow should be pointing *down* towards the shuttle.

The forward swing is a sweeping action, down and underneath the shuttle, to hit with a straight arm. On impact, in front of and to the left of the leading foot, a strong flick with the wrist will ensure the shuttle travels high. See Fig. 13.

Fig. 13. Underarm Backhand Clear. Jim Sydie really gets down to it.

In both backhand and forehand shots it is important to develop a good backswing as, by so doing, you will allow a strong shoulder and body movement to increase the power. And in any case, if you ran into the net with your racket outstretched, you could play only a weak shot—and your opponent would realise this. With a backswing you have a choice of a strong shot or, by checking the action, a net reply.

NET SHOTS

The underarm clear is the *defensive* answer to a low shuttle in the net area but a more *attacking* reply would be to drop the shuttle just over the net, so forcing your opponent to do the lifting. To do this accurately, so that the shuttle just skims the tape and topples over the other side of the net, requires considerable skill and control. It will help if you take a slightly firmer grip of the racket and restrict the wrist movement somewhat. You must watch the shuttle right on to the strings, and with a firm pushing action direct the shuttle to the spot you have chosen. It will need even less power than for the short service. If the enemy is not lurking near the net and you have room to manœuvre, a straight reply will be best but otherwise, and particularly if the shuttle is very close to the net, play it across, i.e. upwards and outwards towards the net posts. Due to the distance the shuttle has to travel you will find this easier to control, but do not get into the habit of crossing all your shots just for the sake of ease. The straight ones are usually more effective.

This describes what you should do when the shuttle has fallen fairly well below the level of the tape. These shots are quite difficult to execute properly. The lower they are taken, the more difficult they are. So, to be effective at the net, and to save yourself a lot of frustration, *play the shuttle early*. Always think in terms of contacting it as high and as near to the tape as possible. If you can meet the shuttle above the height of the net, your intention *must* be to hit down.

There will be no time for any appreciable backswing and so, when you first practise net play, content yourself with just 'blocking' the shuttle. If you do make contact above the tape, the shuttle will 'die' and drop steeply downwards over the net. After a while, when you realise that you can get there early enough, bring in a wrist action to snap the shuttle smartly down. Try pushing the shuttle—but to an open space, not on to the opposition's racket! The follow through is virtually non-existent, indeed this tendency must be checked to avoid touching the net. See Fig. 14.

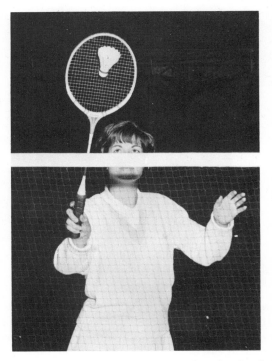

Fig. 14. The 'Dab' or 'Push' at the net, showing the shuttle being hit BEFORE it falls too low, with the player's racket IN FRONT OF HER.

Obviously there are going to be times when the shuttle cannot be met early enough and on these occasions you will have to accept that you cannot hit down. You will have to alter your intention rapidly and, before the shuttle can drop too low, drop the racket head underneath it and with a very gentle forward and upward push, endeavour to pop it over the net at tape height. See Fig. 15.

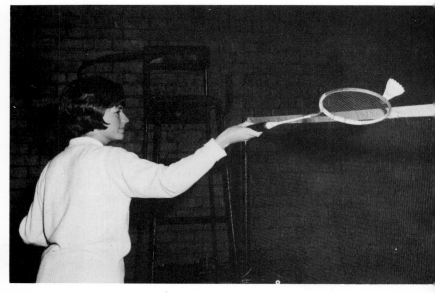

Fig. 15. A Net Shot showing the angle of the racket in order to just make the shuttle trickle over the other side of the net.

The only way you can have a reasonable chance of taking the shuttle as it crosses the net is, first of all, to look for and anticipate what is coming. Next, you must *hold your racket up*, in front of you, at tape height. The other vital essential is that you must be on your toes, knees bent with a bit of 'bounce' in your legs. Make sure that you are close enough to deal with the shots in front of you, but not so close as to hamper your movement.

Net play is a fine art, and can be great fun, but do not indulge in duels. Concentrate on getting to the shuttle early and putting it down.

RETURN TO A SMASH

Your aim in returning a smash is to play the shuttle into your opponent's court, *in such a way that he will have difficulty in making a good reply*—which is all very well to write about, but often so difficult to put into practice. You must accept that if you put the shuttle in the air you are inviting a smash and if your length is poor, you are in trouble. True, he could drop shot or clear, in which case you will have to move smartly, but the main consideration is the possible smash.

Prepare for this by adopting an open stance, biased towards the backhand with your right foot just in the lead. Bend your knees slightly and keep on the balls of your feet. You cannot afford to be glued to the floor, for you will have to move rapidly if your opponent does not smash. With a backhand grip, bring the racket across your body, with its head opposite your left shoulder. Keep the racket head up because I want you to move into the smash and take it early. You will not be able to do this at first and will probably feel happier if you stand mid-court. However, with experience and as your timing improves, move forward and try to take the shuttle earlier and higher.

There will not be much time for an appreciable backswing but with the racket held up, you are half-way there. The forward action will depend on how high you can take the shuttle and the type of stroke selected. For the lob to the back of the court, the action will be just as in your underarm clear, apart from the limited backswing and, owing to this, more wrist movement will be needed.

At first, this will be your most common return, but you

must appreciate that with this shot, you are merely putting the shuttle back up in the air. So, unless the opposition is standing there, a drop shot just over the net would be more effective as a rule. You should play this drop shot rather like your drives although, again, you won't have the backswing, and your wrist action will have to be checked to slow down the shuttle. It will probably go a little high at first, but with practice your timing and touch will improve so that you will be able to pop the shuttle just over the net.

If the smashed shuttle is travelling on a flat path, a very effective reply is to drive it back. This is executed just like your normal drive, which is another point in favour of having the racket head up. You will need a good backswing in order to get the power behind your shot. This power, combined with the speed of the shuttle makes the drive return to a smash a very formidable shot. You will have to 'get your eye in' and play the shuttle early for the shot to be fully effective.

The whole secret of any of these returns to a smash is not to be afraid of the shuttle. Do not let it come to you; go forward to meet it.

ROUND-THE-HEAD

A 'round-the-head' stroke is peculiar to badminton and, as its name implies, is played with the forehand face of the racket—but on the backhand side of the body. This is achieved by arching the back and bending the body sideways, to the left. To maintain balance it will be necessary to move the left foot further to the left than for a normal forehand stroke.

Refer to Fig. 16 to see what you should look like immediately before you hit the shuttle and then practise the stroke in this way. Have a friend feed the shuttle high to you, to pass over your left shoulder. Prepare to make a normal forehand stroke, so your racket is in the back-scratching position.

Fig. 16. Round-the-Head Smash. Notice the arched back, the weight on the left foot, the racket arm almost brushing the top of the head.

Then, instead of the swing upwards to make contact with the shuttle on the right hand side of the body, sweep your arm across the top of your head so that the forehand face of the racket meets the shuttle. You will appreciate that your arm must be bent, as you hit the shuttle at a point beyond your left shoulder.

The action may seem rather strange at first but, if you persevere, it will become quite natural. You will learn just how far you must move your left foot to the side in order to position yourself correctly. Also, you will discover various points of contact. For instance, for a cross-court shot, the shuttle will usually be hit slightly in front of the body, whereas, for a straight shot, the point of contact would be better alongside the head or behind it.

As you make the stroke your weight will be on your left foot and after hitting there will be a tendency to overbalance. The more to the left you play the shot the more likely you are to overbalance in that direction. You must therefore concentrate on a rapid recovery, or you will have problems in getting to the next shot.

The wrist, again, plays a vital part in the effectiveness of this stroke as it should put a crisp snap into the shot to help compensate for the absence of body weight going *into* the shot.

The smash is the most usual stroke played round-the-head but, of course, the clear and the drop can be executed in this way too. If overplayed the round-the-head smash can be tiring (owing to the twisting of the body and the extra footwork necessary to get round to it), and recovery from it is not as easy as with the normal forehand shot. However, despite these possible disadvantages, I would always recommend it as a more aggressive stroke than one of the backhand shots.

Part Four: TACTICS

There is nothing very complicated about the strategy of badminton. It is largely a matter of common sense. You want to win, and therefore you must play the sequence of strokes most likely to force your opponent to make an error or present you with an opening so that you are able to kill the shuttle. Ideally, you should have a range of strokes which will enable you to deal competently with the shuttle under all circumstances. Ranking equally in importance with stroke play is movement. I have already stressed this earlier and, as you will find in a hard game, the value of quick, correct movement cannot be overestimated. Unless you can move well into position and execute a good stroke when you get there, all preconceived plans are useless.

Although you will not have fully mastered movement and strokes and will still have difficulty in doing all you want to do, this does not prevent you from employing the other vital ingredient of tactics, *Thought*! As soon as you learn to play a simple rally, start to think about the game. Do not be content just to return the shuttle over the net, do so with a purpose. Play the shuttle back, but aim for a particular spot with the object of making it difficult for your opponent to return. Think about his strong points and his weaknesses. Has he got a weak backhand? Has he got a hard smash? Can he reach my drop shots?

Apart from your opponent, think about yourself. Look at yourself honestly, and assess what you are good at and what you are not so good at. In the latter case, decide you are going to work harder at this feature to bring yourself up to scratch. Discover the sort of shots you must play to stop your opponent exploiting your weaknesses and the kind of strokes that can make him play to your strong points. If you can learn to analyse your opponent and yourself in this way, you will be able to arrange your strokes to bring about the reply you want. A good rule to remember is: *play to his weakness; make him play to your strength.*

In addition to this analysis of the players, you must learn to look for the spaces on court, on both sides of the net. These are the spots to aim for in your opponent's court. If you can play a good shot into a space, he may never reach it, but even if he does, you have at least made him run and it is very difficult to play a winning shot on the move. But don't forget the gaps in your own court. Try to be aware of the spaces you have created and do your best to fill them, otherwise they offer obvious targets to your opponent and you could be forced into making a weak return if he used them.

When discussing the tactics of badminton there is an expression which keeps cropping up, the *Angle of Return*. This really refers to the path along which it is possible to direct the shuttle in relation to the width of the court. The diagrams will help to show what I mean. Fig. 17 illustrates a *narrow* angle of return. 'A' has played a shot high to the centre of the opposing court, and the lines show the widest paths the shuttle can take to pass him. By positioning himself centrally, 'A' cuts down the angle and is equidistant from the points at which he could intercept the shuttle on either wing.

Fig. 18 shows a *wide* angle of return. This time 'A' has played his shot from the backhand tram-line, cross-court, deep into his opponent's backhand corner, and you can see the very wide angle created and the distance 'A'

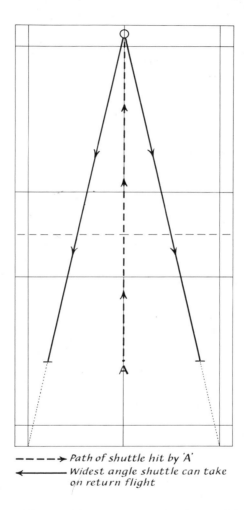

Path of shuttle hit by 'A'
Widest angle shuttle can take
on return flight

Fig. 17. Diagram illustrating a Narrow Angle of Return.

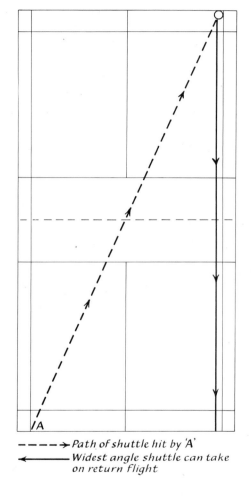

----→ *Path of shuttle hit by* 'A'
←———— *Widest angle shuttle can take on return flight*

Fig. 18. Diagram illustrating a Wide Angle of Return.

will have to travel to intercept the shuttle if it is played straight to his forehand corner.

This shows the theory of the angle of return at its simplest. It is applicable to every shot played in badminton, although other factors will influence the base you adopt, such as time and pace. Do not worry too much about this for the moment, I mentioned it mainly so that you will understand what I mean when I use the expression later. All it really means is watching very carefully when you do a cross-court shot that you haven't left a wide open space and an easy shot for your opponent to score a winner. When you are playing you will not, at first, have time to consider these details, but I would certainly recommend you to watch other games or even work out some sequences on paper. I am sure you will benefit if you can grasp that, although from a given position it is possible to direct the shuttle along a number of paths, it is also possible to calculate the quickest and the slowest path and therefore the best base to adopt to deal with possible returns.

These are some of the fundamentals upon which sound strategy is based, and they are common to all branches of the game. I would now like you to look more specifically at the different games which make up the family of bad-minton. Please read ALL the parts, even if you do not think that part concerns you. To save boring repetition, I only deal in detail with an important feature the first time I refer to it, and when it is applicable to another section I shall merely draw your attention to it. Of course, there are techniques I may suggest in one game which may be used to advantage in another game and, naturally, I would expect you to apply and adapt these techniques as you see fit.

Tactics are very personal and so I have set out to work on only general lines. From any given situation there are pro-bably dozens of different answers and it would be impossible for me to cover even half of them. Indeed if I tried to do so, I would be doing you a grave disservice, for I believe that you can only become a good tactician if you can think and work out the strategy which suits you. The following pages will give you a good base to start from, since they deal both with the fundamentals of each game and with some of the more common situations you will find. From there you must then think, scheme and explore yourself.

SINGLES

The game of singles is fundamentally the same for both men and ladies and so, for discussing the *basic* game, I shall draw no distinction between the sexes. For so many players, in England anyway, the true game of singles is difficult to practise as the very nature of the game demands considerable height above the net. The top class player would expect to be able to hit the shuttle to a height of 30 feet, particularly on his service, and not many halls will permit this. Be that as it may, do not let the lack of height prevent you from experimenting with the singles game, for the obstructions you encounter will merely mean that you will have to adapt your strokes accordingly.

If you look at the singles court you will notice that the side tram-lines have been removed and the serving area extended to the base line. So now you have a long, narrow court and this determines the type of game you will play and the base you occupy in order to defend it. 'Base' is very important: it refers to the position on court to which you should always return immediately you have played your shot—no matter from which part of the court you played that shot.

Roughly speaking your base will be in the centre of your court, about 6 feet behind the short service line and over the centre line. Depending on your opponent's play and your own ability to move, you will find that you can alter this base in a fore and aft direction. It is easier to move forwards than to move backwards and you may be tempted to adopt a deep base—particularly if you are a lady. However, you must

Ladies' Singles. An all-Japanese Final at the All-England Championships, with Miss Yuki on base ready to deal with whatever comes. Miss Takagi left this shot to her deep backhand rather late, but still managed to get it back.

also consider that it takes the shuttle longer to travel in a high arc to the back of the court than it takes to travel downwards to the forecourt, as in a drop shot. Therefore, if you do take up a position deep in court, you must be aware of the opening you offer for the front of the court to be attacked.

During the course of play you will soon learn to adapt your base according to the style of play of your opponent and the effect of your own shots. For instance, if your opponent is constantly playing clears to within inches of your base line and you have difficulty in getting behind these shots, you

Men's Singles. An exciting rally from which it is obvious that AKIYAMA doesn't believe in backhand clears whilst he is still able to put the pressure on. Tan Aik Huang is beautifully poised to intercept the shuttle—which he did.

will have to move a little farther back. However, this is exactly what he wants and, when he finds that he has you pinned to your base line, he will produce his drops and smashes to attack the openings you have left at the front. Equally, if you manage to do the same to him and force him to play poor length shots, you may then move your base nearer to the net.

When thinking of your base in relation to the width of the court you must consider the angle of return and position yourself so that you will be equidistant from the possible points of interception.

Base is very important but, until you become experienced, you will find that always returning to the centre of your court will hold you in good stead. The main thing to remember is that when you have played your shot you must move off straight away. To stand looking after it will mean that you will be late for the next shot you have to play and this will result in your scurrying about the court playing desperation shots.

So much for your base during a rally; but it is important for you to get off to the right start with your service. You will see that it will be best for you to serve from a position that will require the minimum amount of movement on your part, after the service has been delivered. Therefore I suggest a position some 4 to 6 feet behind the short service line and as near as permissible to the centre line. After the shuttle has been struck you need then only take one step to the side in order to straddle the centre line and there you are on base.

When receiving service I recommend a position about 4 feet behind the short service line and approximately 3 feet from the centre line, or, in other words, roughly in the centre of the court. I am sure this would be best for you in the left-hand court although, when receiving in the right-hand court you may feel happier about your backhand if you stood nearer to the centre line. This should enable you to cope with most services, but if you find you are being caught out you must make whatever adjustment is necessary to meet the situation.

The idea in singles is to manœuvre the opposition away from his base, create an opening in his court and make him present you with a weak return which you can kill. In view of the court dimensions you will appreciate that you will best achieve this by exploiting the length of the court and, with this in mind, your basic service should be the high one—as high and as deep as possible. A shuttle landing vertically on the base line is very difficult to time, for it lacks pace and therefore needs more power to return it full length. It also means that the player will be forced to the extreme limit of the court in order to play the shot.

Usually your service should be directed to the centre of the opponent's court—to cut down the angle of return. By all means try services to the side lines, but when you do, you will need to take a step nearer to that side. By so doing you will narrow the angle and place yourself nearer the obvious reply, the straight.

The other service variants may be tried, but with caution. A flick does not have much effect, as a rule, due to the receiver being so far back in court. A drive can be very dangerous if intercepted. The short service is often useful, particularly against an opponent who has started to anticipate a high shot. Take care when you do use it. If the opponent can meet the shuttle early, he can dribble it over the net, push it to a space or flick it over your head. You will just have to experiment to find out which type of service produces the best results against that particular opponent.

When you receive a high service, the situation is just the same as when you receive a high clear during a rally and therefore the tactical considerations are the same. As the shuttle comes to you, note your opponent's position on court, decide what is the best shot to play and then play it to the best of your ability. The permutations are endless and I can only offer very general advice.

The first principle in a game must be to keep the shuttle in play. By this I do not mean 'stonewalling', being content just to get the shuttle back over the net and wait for the opponent to make a mistake. On the contrary, take the initiative, attack, but with control. You have a great deal of court at your disposal, so do keep the shuttle inside the lines and get it over the net. Until you are quite sure of your touch and accuracy, aim to play a few inches inside the lines. When playing shots to the net, unless the opponent is standing there, allow some margin for error. Rarely does the shuttle need to crawl over.

There will be very little time to decide which shot is the best to play and your selection will depend on certain considerations. If your opponent has left a big space in his court, this will probably be your first choice. If the space is in the forecourt area, a downward stroke is indicated, your smash if you are in a good position or, alternatively, a half-smash or a drop shot. To *attack* a space in the back court, a fast clear travelling on a low trajectory could prove very difficult to return. Against an opponent who is well positioned and who has no obvious gaps there are two alternatives. If he has a known weakness, like a weak backhand or is very slow in coming in to the net, this will indicate the best spot to aim for. If no weakness is apparent you will have to probe deeper and use a safe shot initially such as a high deep clear, preferably to a corner.

Most players are suspect in their deep backhand corner and this is the area I would probe first, particularly if I wanted to play a safe shot. Mind you, plugging the backhand can be overdone and if you find your attack to this corner is not causing undue stress to your opponent, switch to some sharp clears deep into his forehand corner. A number of players, probably feeling secure, often get to this shot late and produce a poor return. The same policy could be followed with the fellow who is constantly biased towards his backhand. A few good length clears deep into the forehand will often show a worthwhile result. Either he will put up a weak reply or he will open up his backhand so much that the weakness he was trying so hard to protect now becomes an easy target.

If you are extremely fit, or playing against very poor opposition, you may find that your are able to create openings with your smash. But if you find that your smashing does not have this effect you will have to think again. It is pointless to continue with a policy of smashing if it merely serves to make you lose position, and possibly your attack. You will just have to face it, either your smash is lacking or

you are up against a very good defence. Check your smashes
at a later date for speed, angle and direction and work at
them. In the meantime you have to get on with the game.

Play the sequence of shots most likely to work your opponent out of position and, when you have made a space, play
your smash then. The faster your shots, the more chance there
is of forcing the opponent to make an error providing you
can keep up the pace yourself. Against a good defensive
player you will find the tendency is that he will be slowing
the game down. He will play all his shots high and deep, he
wants to create time. Don't allow him to do so. Speed the
game up. If he has to answer a fast shot there is a good chance
that the height and depth which is so important to him will
be denied him, he will then start to make mistakes. By the
same token, if he likes fast rallies, try to slow them down with
your high shots and very tight drop shots. You should always
be thinking of the sort of game YOU want to play, how you can
do this and prevent your opponent from playing the sort of
game HE wants to play.

The sequence of shots you play in your opening-up process
is important. If you played the first shot to the base line and
the next tight to the net, you would make your opponent cover
the greatest distance but, if this pattern were reproduced too
frequently, it would not be too great an effort for him
to trot backwards and forwards. However, if you broke up the
sequence so that he did not know what sort of shot you were
going to play next, he would not be able to move so fluently.
He would be apt to pause in between strokes and any weakness would soon become evident. So, mix up your shots, and
keep him guessing all the time.

Instead of clear, drop, clear, etc., you could try, for
example, clear, clear, clear, drop. Or, clear, drop, clear,
smash, and so on. To this variation in the sequence of your
shots add deception, and you will make life very difficult
for your opponent. By deception I mean making the initial
preparation for the same group of shots look the same.

Remember, in the strokes section I stressed the importance of
making your clear, smash and drop look the same. Try also
not to play your shots at the same pace. Alternate a slow
drop with the fast. Clear the shuttle at different speeds and
different trajectories. Instead of always doing a full-blooded
smash, throw in a steeply angled smash which whilst not
travelling so fast falls nearer to the net.

This is all very well whilst you are in control of the situation, but it's not so smart when you are having a taste of
your own medicine. The ability to anticipate where the
next shot is to be played is of tremendous value. To this end
you must, very soon after the game has started, discover
if the opponent has a favourite shot or can be expected to
play a particular shot in a certain situation. At the same time
you must be on your toes, ready to move immediately you
have seen where the shuttle is going. Watch the shuttle right
on to his racket.

Be on your guard against the drop shots. You must take
them early. The fast variety will almost certainly fall beyond
the short service line and it is the speed of these shots which
will beat you. However, if you are on your base, you should
be able to get to them. More often than not the fast drops
are played cross-court and therefore your usual answer will
be a straight shot. The slow drop is intended to hug the net.
If it does and it is allowed to fall, you will be in trouble.
You must do your best to meet it as soon as it crosses the
tape. If you can do this you will then have the choice of
either just dabbing it over the net or flicking it over your
opponent's head, and the tables will have been turned on him.

Cross-court shots are not taboo, but do watch when and
where you use them. They have the longest distance to
travel and so take the longest time to reach their destination,
which is a feature you *might* make use of if you are trying to
gain time. The main danger of any cross-court shot is that if
the opponent can intercept it early, he can put the shuttle
smartly away straight down a line, the farthest distance from

you. This particularly applies if your opponent is moving towards the intended path of the shuttle. Concentrate on playing the bulk of your shots straight, reserving the cross-courts for the occasions when you have well and truly pushed your opponent out of position.

There is much room for deception in the singles game, and one occasion when you are likely to be caught out is when you move in a certain direction just as your opponent is making his stroke. Without too much difficulty he can direct the shuttle in the opposite direction and you will have quite a job stopping, twisting and rushing off the other way. To avoid this uncomfortable situation you must always try to be ready, anticipating the next shot. Whenever possible play your shots to give yourself time to regain your position and balance so that you are not on the move WHEN YOUR OPPONENT STRIKES THE SHUTTLE—or at any rate not moving fast.

Whenever you are in doubt or when you are in trouble, play a safe shot. Play it high and deep, preferably straight and to a corner.

Do play singles, whatever your facilities and whatever your ability. It is a physically and mentally demanding game, but it is the best way to make rapid progress, and it can be great fun.

MIXED DOUBLES

Amongst sociable badminton players this is the most popular but, unfortunately, the most misused of the games. There are certain gentlemen I have encountered who use this medium as a means to enjoy a game of singles with the opposing man, while leaving their female partners to develop a grand inferiority complex, and a severe cold. Mixed doubles, to be successful, must be a true partnership in every sense of the word. Each partner, whilst fulfilling a different function, works to the same end by using his and her particular talents to the common good of the team.

Mixed Doubles. An all-England Derby at the 'All-England' between two of the finest pairs in the world. The immaculate backhand drive is being executed by Tony Jordan, ably assisted by Susan Whetnall. But woe betide him if he crosses that shot on to Gillian Perrin's waiting and expectant racket. Roger Mills, nimble as ever, looks capable of coping with a shot to any other part of the court.

The key-note is ATTACK. To attack effectively the players must position themselves with this thought uppermost in their minds and that is why the 'front and back' system is generally adopted. The lady should be at the front of the court and be responsible for the whole width of the court between the net and the front service line; the man covers the remainder. The reasoning behind this is that the man, usually, is stronger and faster than his partner and is therefore more capable of dealing with the 'heavy' work at the back. The lady, because she *usually* lacks power deep in court and because she generally has a more delicate touch, is better suited to fill the net role.

Do not let it be thought that the lady has the easier task, far from it. Because the shuttle reaches her much more quickly than it does the man behind her, she has a very limited time to react and deal with the shot. So it does not help when the partner behind pops the shuttle into the air and she has to steel herself for the full-blooded smash invariably aimed straight at her, combined with the cry 'Why don't you stay up at the net?' Nor does it help when her partner indulges in a cross-court slashing contest. With the shuttle whistling about her ears, the poor girl obviously cannot anticipate anything—she just gets dizzy. I hope any erring male readers will study this paragraph again.

I am not saying that all the fault lies with the man. The lady, by her intervention at an untimely moment, will often thwart the carefully laid plans of her partner. She must remember that the man has longer to see the shuttle and, if he's a reasonable player, will not be far from her and so can usually get to a shot which is just out of her reach. It is quite true to say that the more shots the lady can take, effectively, the more pressure she can place on the opposition and take off her partner, but, until she is quite experienced, the lady should content herself by playing only those shots in front and to the side of her, *that she can control*.

Let us examine the roles of the players, what they are each trying to achieve and how they combine to become an effective team.

For You Both

Accept what I have said about the front and back system. Try other methods by all means but, unless you are faced with rather poor opposition, you will find that the lady simply cannot play on an equal footing with the man as, for example, in a 'sides' formation. She will just attract all the attacking shots from the opponents and must eventually crack under the barrage.

You are seeking to attack, and the front and back is the strongest system in attack; BUT it is the weakest in defence. You can see why if you look at Fig. 19, which shows the suggested starting positions for the players to serve and receive service. The main gaps on the court are down the sides, presenting ideal openings for an attacking stroke. So a most important feature of your game must be to play the shuttle downwards, or at worst flat, whenever possible. On the occasions that you do have to play a clear, it must be high and deep to the spaces at the back.

You will almost certainly be playing against the same sort of formation, and so the man will use drives, smashes and drop shots to probe the gaps in the opposing court. Initially he will be trying to create an opening, to force one or other of the other team to lift the shuttle and, when this happens, he will play his killing shot. The lady, by her positioning in the forecourt, hopes to discourage the opposition from playing anything to the net and thereby induces them to lift the shuttle to her partner. When the shuttle does come her way, she will play whatever shot she considers best to further her side's attacking policy, e.g. steep pushes, net shots and stop shots (i.e. blocking a fast moving shuttle by holding her racket in its path).

There is nothing rigid or fixed about this front and back system. It is a general policy designed to suit the physical capabilities of the parties and emphasise attack. It is not true to say that *everything* at the front is the lady's and *everything* at the back is the man's. There must be occasions when one partner will have to move from his/her normal sphere of operation to help out the other when in trouble—but only when in trouble. If either partner makes a habit of 'poaching' on the other's territory, it will soon be noticed by the enemy and used to your disadvantage. The same reasoning applies to

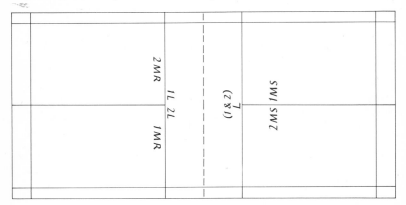

Lady Receiving. ɪʟʀ: Lady's position when receiving in right-hand court. 2ʟʀ: Lady's position when receiving in left-hand court. ɪᴍ: Man's position for ɪʟʀ. 2ᴍ: Man's position for 2ʟʀ.

Lady Serving. ɪʟs: Lady's serving position from right-hand court. 2ʟs: Lady's serving position from left-hand court. ᴍ(ɪ and 2): Man's position for ɪʟs and 2ʟs.

Man Receiving. ɪᴍʀ: Man's position when receiving in right-hand court. 2ᴍʀ: Man's position when receiving in left-hand court. ɪʟ: Lady's position for ɪᴍʀ. 2ʟ: Lady's position for 2 ᴍʀ.

Man Serving. ɪᴍs: Man's position when serving from right-hand court. 2ᴍs: Man's position when serving from left-hand court. ʟ(ɪ and 2): Lady's position for ɪᴍs and 2ᴍs.

Fig. 19. Positions for Serving and Receiving in Mixed Doubles.

the suggested positions for serving and receiving. These are the best positions in the majority of cases, but can of course be varied to suit individual needs.

For The Lady

The finest weapon you can possess for the mixed doubles game is, without doubt, a good short service. Armed with this both you and your partner know that the attack from the opponents has been minimised, that, unless they are of very high calibre, they can do little else but lift the shuttle. You are thus able to concentrate all your attention on any net return and your partner on any shot lifted higher. If your short service is not good, the gaps I mentioned are an easy target for a rushed return, which means that your side will immediately be on the defensive.

So a good basic short serve is your first consideration, but don't forget the variations you can use. If your lady opponent is standing well back in court she should be able to cope with a flick service and so, in this case, the short serve is best until she has been brought forward. A high service to the lady is always worth trying. If she is slow at moving back, she may play a weak return and may well be slow in moving back to the net again. Your partner should be able to capitalise on both these counts. However, do watch out for this lady's drop shot or smash.

To the man, a short service is a must. Apart from getting him to lift the shuttle, you should also be thinking about drawing him in to the net in the hope that you will then be able to flick the shuttle over his head into the back court. Of course, some men are very good at rushing the services and this is where your flick really comes into its own. Don't do it every time or the element of surprise will be lost, but its judicious use should keep the aggressive man guessing and less eager to try his devastating rush. I would not recommend serving high to a man—not unless you want to come to a sticky end.

Immediately you have played your short or flick service you must move forwards. Ideally you should move also in the direction you anticipate a net reply, but this will be difficult until you have gained experience. If you move forwards, you

will be in a better position to deal *early* with any net returns
and, if the service is rushed, you will be out of the way and
so give your partner a better chance to retrieve the shuttle.
You would therefore be well advised to serve from as near to
the junction of the short service and centre lines as possible.
You will be nearer the net, the opposition will have less time
to see your service coming and you will allow your partner
to take up his position well into the forecourt area. (This is
very important to him.)

When receiving service you cannot afford to 'toe' the line
because of the danger of the flick and the high services.
Instead, I suggest you stand 2 to 3 feet behind the short
service line and about a foot away from the centre service
line. (You will have to work out what is the best position for
you against the particular opponents.) This position should
give you ample time to move back, BUT you must be prepared to move rapidly forwards on a short service so that
you can take it before the shuttle drops too low. With
practice, you will be able to meet it early enough just to tip
the shuttle over the tape. As your experience and confidence
grows you should be able to attack all but the very best services. If you can meet the shuttle high enough, you should hit
it steeply downwards into the forecourt or, if the man's
position permits, fast and straight down a side line.

The flicks and the high services could cause you some
trouble. How well you can deal with them will depend on
how well and how quickly you can move backwards. Your
aim must still be to attack, if you can, and therefore your best
replies are the smash or drop shot—to the spaces. If you are
forced to do a clear, make it very high and deep. No matter
what your reply to a high shot (whether it be on service or
during a rally) your partner would, as a rule, prefer you to
regain your position in the net area *immediately* you have
played it. Unless you do, the enemy will have scored a tactical
victory by placing both you and your partner in your weakest
positions. You will find yourself pinned to the back line and

will have to play out the remainder of the rally. Which is
not a rosy prospect! I said 'as a rule'. If you really can cope
at the back for the occasional rally, and you and your
partner have agreed on this, then I wish you luck, for you
should be a very strong couple.'

Once the rally is in progress and you are in your normal
forward position, you will need to be on your toes and be
prepared to skip along the length of the net as the play
moves from side to side. You should try to position yourself
so that you can meet and control any straight shot as soon as
it crosses the net, whilst at the same time guarding against a
possible cross-court shot to the net. Most of your shots will be
wristy dabs as you will not have time to swing the racket head
at the shuttle, and so it is vital that you hold your racket
up in front of you all the time the shuttle is in play. Learn
to anticipate the replies, look for the obvious shots the
opponents will try and keep the racket up ready to intercept
the shuttle as soon as it crosses the tape. See Fig. 20.

Play your shots very steeply down, or quickly past and
away from the man. You need not always hit the shuttle
hard, in fact speed could be used against you. If you can
just dribble the shuttle over the net, this can be a very good
shot; all your opponent can do is lift it. Take care with
'pushed' shots. The best place for these is the spot just behind
the lady and in front of the man. This is quite a difficult
shot to place accurately, and unless it is going downward,
the lady could cut it off to your detriment. The half-court
push can be very dangerous if the man is well positioned,
as he should be able to intercept it without too much trouble
and send the shuttle speeding straight down the line.

When your side is on the attack, you will apply even more
pressure if you can be really well up to the net. You can afford
to do this as your side's shots are going down and are fast,
whereas the opponents' will be rising and slower. These are
the shots you have been waiting for, take advantage of the
situation and kill them. *Do not push them back into play.*

Fig. 20. The Lady's position at the net. Racket up. Good balance—on her toes, ready to deal with anything along the net.

When you are defending, exactly the opposite occurs, and to give yourself more time, it will help to drop back a little— but not too far, on the short service line should be about right. Even though you now have to defend, you should still be thinking about getting back on the attack and to do that one of you will have to intercept the shuttle and hit it *downwards*. If you can do this, your partner will bless you, but you must exercise caution. It will be very tempting to try to intercept a fast shot, but unless you can control it, don't do it. Leave it to your partner.

There are going to be times when your team puts the shuttle into the air in the opponent's court and when this happens a lot of men are going to choose you as their target. This can be a terrifying moment but, if you hold the racket in front of your face, no harm can come to you. So, don't scuttle backwards, hold your racket up in front of you in a pan-handle grip and line up the face of the racket in the anticipated path of the shuttle. Choose, if you can, a position diagonally opposite to the attacker, as this will give you more time to see the shuttle. You will usually find it better to adopt a semi-crouching position so that the face of the racket is about level with the top of the net. Watch the flight of the shuttle. If it's aimed straight for your head it will not be too difficult but, if it is to a side, you will have to adjust the position of your racket. At first you will have difficulty but, when you get your eye in, I don't think you will find this defence too hard. A 'stop-shot' will be quite effective and as you become more skilled at this, you will find that you can actually smash back a smash, and that will really upset your opponent.

For The Man

As you have to defend the back court and as there is no need for you to follow your service into the net, your serving position will be deeper in court than your lady's, perhaps 4 feet from the short service line but as close to the centre

service line as possible. Again this is not a fixed rule and must
be varied to suit you. You must weigh up the pros and cons.
The farther back you stand, the flatter you should be able to
guide the shuttle, but the more time you are allowing your
opponent to follow the shuttle. Therefore, if you allow too
much time, you risk the early interception of your service and
you will have created gaps in the danger area between you
and your lady. If you stand very near to the short service
line, you are reducing the time factor, but you are creating
a large space at the back of the court whch is very inviting for
a flick over your head. You will have to work out the best
position for you, in relation to the ability of your opponents.

Your serving policy will be very like your partner's. The
short serve should be the basic and, as far as serving to the
man is concerned, you should serve largely to the centre of
the court. A careful use of flick services to the man and high
services to the lady will keep them both guessing and will
help to ease the pressure on your service.

Having served, you must be instantly ready to move to
cover a large area. As well as the width of the court, you also
have about 16 feet depth to look after. Your opponents will
be doing their best to hit the shuttle down into this vast
space and your task is to intercept the shuttle before it has
fallen much below the level of the tape and play a similar
shot against them. Quite a difficult task at best, but impossible if you delay and so you must never let the shuttle come
to you. You must always think of going forward to meet it.

Just as in singles, you have a base. In the mixed game this
is roughly in the centre of the court, over the centre service
line and about 4 to 8 feet behind the short service line. Just
where will again depend very largely on your ability. If you
find that you are continually stretching forwards to pick up
half-court shots from near the floor, you can be sure that
you are standing too deep. The more you can approach the
forecourt, the earlier you can reach the shuttle and the more
you can narrow the angle of your opponent's return. Try

hard, then, to press forwards. Try to play the shuttle, not at your side but diagonally forwards.

Your stance to receive service will be just the same as for men's doubles. If the service is high or flicked it can certainly be hit downwards as you have a partner standing there waiting for the return. Smash to the side or to the centre of the court depending on the most likely looking space, and look out for a fast cross-court drive in reply. The same applies to drop shots, bearing in mind that there is probably a lady standing there with her racket up.

The drive should be the main stroke you will use in mixed doubles. I say 'should be' because I assume that your opposing man will be playing as sensibly as you and he will also be doing his best to keep the shuttle down. Hence, you will both be trying to make your openings with the flat shots. Should this not be the case and you find the shuttle being lifted to you, do not hesitate to smash it. You can make the opponents lift the shuttle either by placing it in front of them below net level, or behind them, in such a manner that they have to reach backwards to play the shot. There are obvious reasons for the method you select, although in the heat of the game, these choices may not appear so obvious.

The shot I mentioned in the lady's section in which the shuttle is placed just behind the lady but in front of the man is also an excellent shot for the man, but it should be a downward stroke. If this is a rising shuttle and slow, the lady will have no trouble in cutting it off. At a faster pace she may try for it, but mis-hit it or, being undecided, leave it for her partner who will probably be late and so be forced to scramble it up.

A shuttle hit sharply down to half-court will make the man lift, but it must be going down. One of these floating things which the man can take waist high is very dangerous as he can do virtually what he likes with it.

The full drive straight down the line into the box at the back is an excellent passing shot when the man has been drawn away from that side of the court. It is also a first class shot to use to rush the shuttle into the body of the opponent, particularly if he is on the move at the time.

You will note that I have only mentioned *straight* shots and this is because I would normally recommend these as your first choice. Of course, you will use cross-court shots for they have great value, but only if used at the right time. Here 'the angle of return' rears its head. If you play your shots wisely, which in the main means the straights, and you remember your base, you can use the angle of return to your advantage. If you think about it, your opponent has two choices when he has to play a shot which you have placed straight down the tram-lines. He can either return it straight, which is the quicker, but both you and your partner should be waiting for it and biased towards that side. Or he can play a cross-court. This shot must pass somewhere near the middle of the net, which is your partner's base and if she misses it you should be able to get it if you have not gone *too* far to the side line. The shuttle must travel more slowly on its cross-court path, which therefore gives you more time to reach it anyway. In this situation, once you do contact the shuttle, you have a wide open court waiting for another straight shot down the other side line. The rally could end there, but even if it does not, your opponent will have had to travel the width of the court to reach the shuttle and so is not in a position to play a really effective stroke.

I have simplified the matter, of course, but I think this example shows on the one hand the danger of untimely cross-courting, and on the other the value of the straight shot. If you give some thought to the business of the angle of return you will soon discover that you can limit the danger points to which a shuttle can be returned from any given position. With this knowledge you will then be able to plan your game to ensure the opposition cannot make use of these spots.

Apart from what has been said above, there is another very

good reason why cross-court shots should be kept to the minimum—your partner. If she is to be of value to you, she must be able to anticipate the most likely shot she will have to play. If she can rely on you playing a straight shot, when one is merited, she can prepare to take the reply. But, if she never knows the sort of shot you are likely to play, if the shuttle is perpetually cross-courted and counter cross-courted, she simply cannot decide which way to move. She has to remain static in the middle of the net, of no help to you at all.

Of course you should use your smash whenever you can, not blindly but with purpose, and either for a space or at the body. Take care if you elect to smash at the lady, she might be quite used to it and if she does get her racket in the way, you will never see the shuttle come back!

A very fast, low clear could be used with effect if you have brought both opposing players well out of position, but I would have thought that if you are able to execute one of these clears, you could smash to better effect.

When in serious trouble you will have to clear defensively and in this case it must be very high and deep in order that you and your partner can sort yourselves out into the best position to deal with the situation. When you are forced into a high clear, make it to a corner, preferably the backhand if you can do this with a straight shot. (See 'Triangular Defence' below).

For You Both, Again

I hope I have managed to convey the sort of game you should be playing as individuals and how you should each play shots to help your partner. That is the secret of mixed doubles. You are not necessarily playing the shots to win the point yourself, but rather playing them to create a situation whereby your partner is able to make a kill. In conclusion I shall mention a few points of interest and importance to you both.

We have already established that in mixed doubles we are largely concerned with the *width* of the court. Please use it. Play the shuttle to the four corners. Have your drives, etc., going down the tram-lines. You will be surprised at the difference it will make if you play the shuttle right out to the sides instead of to mid-court.

Consider the pace of the shot you play. So many players hit the shuttle as hard as they can, all the time. This is often unnecessary and the pace can frequently be used against you. The harder you hit the shuttle, the faster it will be returned if a player gets to it. So, when you do hit the shuttle hard, it is wise to make sure that one of you is in a position to deal with a return. Try to establish a regular partnership. In this way you will be able to work out exactly which shots each of you is capable of, which shots you are each able to cover and which shots you are each NOT able to cover. On the question of pace, as I have said before, there is a danger of a very quick cross-court reply in answer to a straight smash from the man at the back. This is an ideal situation for you to work on. Try it out during games and find out if the lady can cope with the cross-court return. Where should she move and just when should she take it and when should she leave it? There are many such sequences you can work on and the more thought you can give to them, the better combination you will get.

You will come across the expression 'triangular or wedge defence'. See Fig. 21. This is the usual system of defence adopted when your team has had to place the shuttle high into the opposing court. The idea is to give the lady at the net more time to see the shuttle's flight and, as we know, the shuttle takes longer to fly diagonally than it does straight. So, when the shuttle is cleared to one corner, the defending lady moves back on to the short service line, about 3 to 4 feet from the centre line, and adopts a stooping stance diagonally opposite the attacking opponent. Her partner's position should be in line with the smasher so that he can deal with the straight smash and probably the straight drop. If the clear is deep, the lady has a very good chance of returning the cross-court smash and drop shot and, if she is very quick, she might even manage the straight drop. This, however, usually falls to the man.

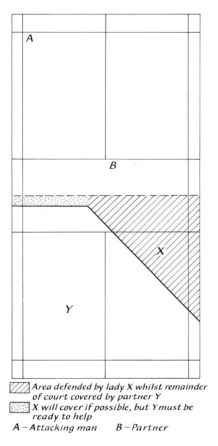

Area defended by lady X whilst remainder of court covered by partner Y

X will cover if possible, but Y must be ready to help

A – Attacking man   B – Partner

Fig. 21. Diagram illustrating the Triangular Defence in Mixed Doubles.

This system is very easy to follow and the beauty of it is that both partners know exactly what is expected of them and what the other is prepared to do. There will be times when the shuttle is sent high, straight down the middle of the court, and when this happens I would recommend that the lady moves to one side or the other so that she can indicate what she expects her partner to deal with.

There will be times when the man is in trouble at the net and then, if she is able, the lady must move back to help out. There will also be many times when the man must take a shot at the net which is not strictly his, but he must take it. How well you cope with these emergencies will depend on the amount of study you have put into your game and the agreements you have reached to deal with them.

During a rally, the man should 'shadow' his partner at all times when there is any doubt in his mind that she will take the shot. In this way he will be ready to play that shot himself should his lady decide fairly late not to do so.

When the lady receives a high or flick service, hits down, and runs in to the net, she should *try* to cover all the net. However, your partnership may have to settle that she is able only to take about half the net—the near half—while her partner must be prepared to get the shuttle back from the other half. Even the best ladies may need this help.

MEN'S DOUBLES

In the men's doubles game the accent is on attack and pace. The frequency with which you can keep the shuttle going down and the understanding you have with your partner will determine your success far more than individual shots.

In singles and mixed you largely had to play for your openings by careful placements and a variation of pace before you could finish off a rally, because, in singles, there is so much ground to cover on your own and, in mixed, you have

Men's Doubles. Illustrating the attacking and defensive formation. Notice particularly the defenders (on the left) have moved partly 'triangular' to cover the anticipated cross-court smash. Ng Boon Bee is giving a wonderful demonstration of a jumping, round-the-head smash—definitely not for the novice!

a partner at the net in a very vulnerable position in front of you. These considerations do not apply to the same extent in men's doubles. Normally you will have a partner of equal strength and ability and between you the whole court can be covered at speed, and any gaps created can be quickly filled. Therefore you can afford to force openings with sheer pace alone. I do not mean that you can throw caution to the winds, of course not, but all your shots should have purpose, and it is most important to keep up a constant pressure on your opponents.

You must try to attack the whole time, never forget this, and I suggest that the front and back formation is the only attacking system you can seriously consider. Some men do adopt a side-by-side formation, which is a system whereby each man looks after his own half court divided by the centre line. He virtually plays a singles in this area. There is no doubt that some partnerships manage quite well in this way —but only at a lower level of play. I think the drawbacks are obvious. Each partner must play a mostly defensive game because even when he smashes he has to rush in to take any weak return at the net, probably arriving rather late. Another strong objection to such a formation is that it should be possible to single out one player and work him into the ground whilst never allowing his partner to hit the shuttle at all.

If you think about it, you should come to the same conclusion that the front and back formation is the best for attack but the side-by-side is the best for defence. This is what the top players have decided and if you wish to progress and enjoy greater success in your men's doubles game, you must adopt the same method.

The idea of switching positions, depending on whether you are attacking or defending, is not difficult to follow, but it often breaks down because the players are slow in adjusting their formation. This is usually due to inexperience in playing a fast game; but quite frequently the shots played are difficult to define as either attacking or defending. Therefore, one man in the team, probably the man at the net, remains rooted to the spot. Do make your shots distinguishable as definite smashes, drops, clears, etc., and avoid these driving contests where brute strength alone decides the issue. In other words, if you keep hitting the shuttle down, rather than flat, your partner will be able to back you up more easily.

A good example of how the system works is to take the case where you have started the rally with a high service.

The receiver will have to move back to intercept the shuttle and, as he does so, his partner must come forward to cover the net area in anticipation of a downward stroke. So they are in a front and back formation and will remain so as long as their team can continue to attack by hitting down. At the same time, because you have offered the attack to your opponent by placing your serve high into his court, you must be prepared to defend and you can do this best by falling back, more or less to the middle of your half court and your partner will do the same alongside you. Thus you and your partner are 'side-by-side' and will have to remain so until you have the opportunity to regain the attack.

If, in this example, the receiver does not hit your high service down, but replies with a clear, he has elected to defend and will move slightly forward whilst his partner will have to come out from the net to a position alongside him into the side-by-side formation. In your team, the man who can most conveniently intercept the shuttle will move back to play the shot whilst his partner goes in to the net. So the roles have been reversed, your side is front and back, and has the opportunity to attack, and I hope you would do so.

This movement 'in' and 'out' MUST BE IMMEDIATE. It is no use watching your partner go back to take a high shot and only moving in to the net when he has played his stroke. That is far too late, as any return played to the net will have fallen well below the level of the tape by the time you reach it. You must move in immediately you appreciate your partner is going back and you should be in an aggressive position at the net *by the time he hits the shuttle*. Conversely, if you have to retreat from the net because one of your side has cleared, you must arrive at your defensive base *before the opponent makes his stroke*.

To start you off on the right track, begin the rally in a front and back formation. Let us look at the serving side first. Everything that has been said under the heading of 'Service' or 'Mixed Doubles' applies, and it would be worth your while to refresh your memory by reading these sections again. You are at the front, about to serve, and the thought uppermost in your mind should be 'What sort of serve must I do to put my side on the attack?' A high one should present no problem to the receiver who will probably smash it, so that's not a good idea. However, if you can direct a short service very close to the top of the net, the receiver will have to lift the shuttle, even if only slightly. This is what you want. This is why you are in the front and back formation to start with.

Remember that as soon as the shuttle leaves your racket you should be moving in to the net. If you do so you should be able to deal with any return from your serve played to the net and, if you take it early, you should be able to put it away. If the receiver rushes the serve and drives the shuttle very fast, because you have moved forward you should not attempt a stroke but should leave it to your partner. He will have a good chance to see and to intercept it. If the receiver lifts the shuttle over your head, that is just what you had hoped for: that is why your partner is standing behind you— to SMASH IT.

Of course, this theory does assume that your service is accurate. One of those things where the shuttle floats six inches above the net is just asking to be hammered. So, brush up on your serving. Think where you are going to stand to deliver the service. If you are up against the centre line you are equidistant from both corners of the net and so, from either the right or the left court, this is where I suggest you stand in relation to the width of the court. As far as your depth in court is concerned, don't forget the points made earlier. The farther away from the short service line you stand, the flatter you should be able to get the shuttle to travel, but there are drawbacks. You will give the receiver more time to see the shuttle. You will have to move farther and therefore faster towards the net after delivering the service in order to take a close return. Your partner will have to take up his position behind you deeper in court. All these pros and cons must be weighed up but your ultimate decision must depend on the position from which you can be most effective.

Having thought about these things look at the receiver and decide which is the best spot in his court to direct your service. Possibly the best serve is the straight, to the junction of the short and centre service lines. This takes the shortest time and it closes the angles through which your opponent can direct his return. However, due to the short distance, this is quite a difficult service to keep flat (more practice needed?) and the receiver does not have to move his racket very much to intercept it. That is why I said you should look at him first and note how he stands to receive. Has he left any obvious gaps? Is he off balance?

Try a service to the 'T' junction first and see how you get on with it. If it is being attacked without difficulty all the time, you will have to think again. Move the service along the front line towards the tram-lines. You have a width of 10 feet to work on and, as a rule, you will find that at some point along this line he will be weak in his interception. Be careful of the service swung very wide right into the tram-lines. If it gets past the receiver it will pay dividends, but, should he be able to meet it early, it will be a simple matter for him to push it straight and deep out of reach of both you and your partner because, as I said before, you will be opening up many possible angles of return.

If, despite these variations in your low service, the receiver is still coming out on top, it means that either he is a very good player or your service is not so good, or both. Now is the time to think about a flick service. Now that he thinks he has your measure, a good flick serve will probably win the point outright but not only that. From this point on he will be more cautious of rushing your service. Thus, with the pressure on your short service eased, you should find it more effective.

If you simply cannot get a decent short service over and your flick doesn't seem to be working either, you are left with the high one. It has its obvious dangers but at least it gets the shuttle into play, and providing you take the appropriate steps to defend you are still in with a chance. But this must be really high and falling vertically on the back service line.

Whilst all this is going on, your partner cannot take a rest. He must be on his toes either to take advantage of your good serves, or dig the side out of trouble after your bad ones. Against the rushed, flat reply he must pick up the shuttle at its highest point and steer it past the opposing front man and out of reach of his partner, that is into the gaps. When you have cleverly made the opposition lift the shuttle high, over your head, he smashes hard and steep into the most vulnerable spot he can detect. Your partner must also be able to cope with those tricky shots which have been pushed just out of your reach and just in front of him. He must meet these early and try to play the stroke that cannot be intercepted by the opponents above net height, so maintaining your attack.

There is a big temptation for the net player to want to 'poach' and take too many shots. Remember the situation is the same as for the lady in mixed doubles. Take only those shots you can control, i.e. hit in front of you or at the side, and never those which have gone behind you (unless, of course, in an emergency when you know that your partner is nowhere near the shuttle).

When you are receiving the service, your first thought is to hit the shuttle down. The receiver can really afford to go all out for attacking the low serves, because he does not have to worry about returning to position at the back of the court immediately as he would in the mixed game. He now has a partner behind him all ready to cope. Stand as near to the short service line as you can with the idea that you are going to meet the shuttle as soon as it crosses the net. Bear in mind that you have to get back to a flick service and still attack this. So, if you find that you are being caught out on the flicks, you will have to compromise and adopt a stance deeper in court. In the right hand court you will probably find that it is best to stand, say, 2 to 3 feet from the centre service line. This will help to protect your backhand against a drive service or a flick. In the left hand court a position roughly mid-court should be suitable. Experiment with the positions and find which suits you best. There will be positions which GENER-ALLY suit you, but be prepared to alter both your position on court and your stance to suit the needs of the moment.

Against a poor low service, rush it and drive it hard into the body of either the server or his partner. Until you are sure of your touch avoid pushing the shuttle at an angle towards the side lines. If at all loose these can easily be picked up and driven hard past you and to your side's disadvantage. Against a service very tight to the net, take it early and dribble it over the net again, either straight, or, if the opponent is there, move it away from him but still close to the net.

If you can deal with the service in this way you will be attacking and so are able to maintain your front and back formation. The usual considerations thus apply. Any return to the net area will be swiftly put away by you and your partner will attack anything returned high to the back of your court.

A high service you should smash. Just as you should a flick service—if you are able. If the flick is deceptive, you will be late in getting to the shuttle and will not be able to do a full-blooded smash. In this case a steep half-smash, angled into the forecourt area, will be equally effective. The alternatives are the drop and clear, in that order. Your endeavour should be always to take a high or flicked service on the forehand, as this enables you usually to be more aggressive than on the backhand. The round-the-head shots come in useful here. Ensure that no one is standing there waiting for your drops and do make sure that your clears go as high as possible and on to the base line. A particular point to ensure is that when you go back to receive a high or flicked service, your partner has moved instantly into the net and has arrived, with racket up at the ready, before you hit the shuttle.

If you can work on this business of serving and receiving and really tighten up in these areas I am sure your game will show a dramatic improvement. What happens immediately after the service will very largely determine the outcome of the rally. If you can do everything I have suggested, again in theory, there will be no rally. Just a service, a return of service, and it's all over. Of course, in practice the shuttle does come back and a rally does take place. Very fast and exciting rallies they can be too, when two evenly matched pairs are battling it out. Just who will win must depend on a number of factors, but I think the most important are those I mentioned in the first paragraph of this section. Have a very clear understanding with your partner and keep the shuttle going down.

When you are attacking at the back of the court, your first choice of stroke must be the smash. Use it and use it as often as possible. But, also use your head! Not all your smashes need be of the same pace. Indeed it would be to your disadvantage if they were all alike, as a wily opponent would soon realise exactly where the shuttle was coming and he would have his racket waiting for it. Vary the pace from the full-blooded affair, through the half smash down to the fast drop shot. Against good opposition there will not be a place for the slow drop unless they are both very foolishly rather far back in the court.

Here again an attacking round-the-head shot played in the backhand corner will usually pay dividends, rather than a weak backhand drop or, worse still, a backhand clear putting your side on the defensive. Recovery is sometimes a problem from round-the-head shots, and the credits and debits of attack with difficult recovery versus defence with easy recovery have to be weighed up, if the stroke is being played from right back in the court and in the corner.

Direct your attack into the gaps. If your opponent is on the move as you are about to strike, either smash at him or at the place he has just left. Against the opponent in a good defensive position you will have to probe for his weakness. Most players defend with a backhand stance. Try smashing close to the forehand side of his body, then on to his backhand. See how he copes with a smash straight at his body. Take care with smashes straight down the tram-lines. These can be fine if there is a known weakness there or no one is near it. However, if you smash on to the racket of a good wristy player, particularly if your trajectory is rather flat, he can do a devastating drive across court and you will then be in hot water.

Despite your good intentions there will be times when you are caught out and cannot effectively do a downward stroke. Rather than place yourself in trouble with a risky shot, clear it. (This applies to shots at the back of the court and shots near the net.) Clear high to the back and so give your partner and yourself the time you will need to take up your defensive side-by-side positions. But think about your game and if you find that you are doing too many of these defensive shots there is something basically wrong. Either your understanding with your partner is at fault or you are too slow in moving into position. So, go back to the fundamentals again.

When it is your turn at the net, your position is exactly the same as the lady's in mixed doubles and you are expected to do the same sort of thing. Fiercer and more aggressive perhaps. Don't play around with the shuttle. Hit it. Hit it down, if you are able, if not, a tight net shot so that the opposition is compelled to lift it to your partner. Do not push the shuttle back into play. Avoid 'floating' shots, these will come whistling back past you. Remember, your partner is playing his shots in such a way that you will be presented with a chance to make a kill. If you cannot finish the rally you must make the shot that will give your partner an opportunity to play a winning stroke. That's what a partnership is all about.

This has assumed that you are always able to attack although, naturally, you will have to defend sometimes. When this happens, do not be content just to accept the inevitable and play the shuttle back, defend with purpose. Scheme to get back on the attack. If you are getting back the smashes from around the region of your ankles or scraping drop shots from off the floor, probably your only reply will be a very high, deep clear. Fairly safe, but you are still offering the enemy another chance at an attacking stroke. Now, if you can get to the shuttle much earlier, you will have a wider variety of shots to play. The flat, fast drive return of a smash mentioned above or, if you can't quite manage this, a faster attacking clear travelling on a lower trajectory than the defensive sort.

The point is that if you are going to defend with these high shots, they must, at least, make the attacker move. If you can return the shuttle fast enough he may attempt another smash off balance and either make a complete mess of it or, at worst, play a weaker shot. If you can drive him into his backhand corner after he has played a shot from the forehand wing he will have to be a very good man indeed to make a winning shot from this position. But, if this defensive tactic is to be successful, you must make him move. You must endeavour to make him play his shots under difficulty, off balance, out of position and you will never do this until you can control your returns of smashes. This means that you MUST MEET THE SHUTTLE EARLY IN FRONT OF YOU.

Apart from high replies, if you can take the shuttle early, you will also be able to consider playing shots to the open spaces in the net area. Or into the space between the man at the net and the attacker in the back court. If you can play this sort of shot and make the opposition meet the

shuttle below the level of the tape, you will have turned the
tables completely and forced them to lift the shuttle to you.

In the situation where you have played a high shot down
the middle of the opponent's court, you and your partner
will have little alternative but to take up a defensive formation side by side and equidistant from the net. But think of
your mixed doubles. You will recall that we argued that it
would be a better arrangement if, when the shuttle went
high to a corner, the partnership adopted a 'triangular' defence.
Why not use the same strategy in your men's game? The
diagonal smash would take longer to reach its intended
destination and so the defender diagonally opposite the
smasher could afford to move in closer to the net. In this
way, if the shuttle came to him, he really could take it very
early and cause great consternation to the enemy. Just how
far this player should move in would depend entirely on his
ability, but you will never know unless you practice and
find out! Naturally, whilst one player moves in to take the
diagonal, his partner will stay further back to deal with the
straight shots and—if previously agreed upon—the cross-
court clear. See Fig. 22.

I hope these few tips on defence will help you, but the best
advice I can give is 'keep up the pressure'. If you can constantly press the opposition and maintain your attack you
will not have to worry too much about your defence.

LADIES' DOUBLES

Modern thinking argues that, as ladies will only have to
play against ladies and, as has already been established in
the men's game, the 'in and out' system is the most advantageous, it is correct for ladies to play in exactly the same way.
I agree. I cannot see any reason why ladies should not play
the same game as the men—PROVIDING THEY CAN DO IT!

I think it must be accepted that ladies do not have the
physical strength or power of men, that they are slower to

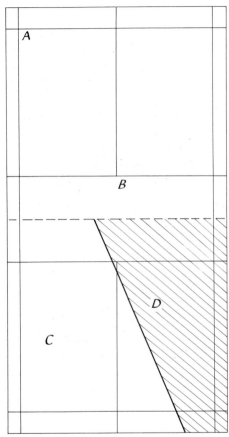

A – The striker   B – Partner
C – Covers clear area
D – Covers shaded area

Fig. 22. Diagram illustrating the Triangular Defence in
Men's and Ladies' Doubles.

Ladies' Doubles. This photograph shows, on the left, a great Japanese pair defending side by side and clearly expecting the attack down the middle, also the very famous partnership of Susan Whetnall and Margaret Boxall rapidly taking up the attacking, front and back formation. At this level the ladies' game is played just like the men's.

cover the court and that their powers of recovery are less— generally speaking, of course. For these reasons alternative methods of play such as side-by-side and round-and-round (as they used to be called) were adopted, but these do not make for a sufficiently attacking game. I always recommend the in and out system—perhaps with modifications—

for ladies starting the game and this is the system I would ask you to follow.

Read through the previous section on men's doubles very carefully and see if you can apply these ideas to your own game. If you are playing against ladies of your own calibre and experience you will probably find the system works very well for you. The acid test will be when you play against a partnership stronger or more experienced than your own. If you should lose, do not discard the system; instead analyse your game to decide why you lost the points, what are the weaknesses in your system and what you must do to put things to right.

Possibly the first thing that will occur to you is that you are not coping very well when your partner makes a low service, follows it in and the receiver rushes the serve back. This is because the situation is foreign to you and the movement and pattern of footwork you have to make is quite different to what you are accustomed in the mixed doubles game. I am afraid there is no easy answer to this. It is just a matter of practice. It would help if four ladies could get together to practice this (and other) likely recurring situations among themselves. Arrange the practice so that your partner always serves low, to the 'T' junction, and the receiver replies with a fast push shot, first to your backhand and then to your forehand. For your part, you must practice the movement necessary to take you into position to play an effective stroke. This is the whole secret—GETTING THERE IN TIME. As your footwork improves you can alter the practice so that the serves are varied and the push replies are also varied.

During a game, watch the receiver's racket very carefully and try to establish, from her stance, the most likely direction she will send the shuttle, so that as soon as she does hit it you can be off the mark and reach the shuttle early. Watching the shuttle off your partner's racket will also help in that. If you can see the direction of the serve, you can sort out in your mind the possible angles of return and so anticipate the most likely return of serve. This, however, is getting a little advanced and you will need a lot of practice before you reach that stage.

When you can get to this pushed return of serve comfortably, reply with another push between the opponents or drive it into the box at the back or, if the net player has left you a space, go for that.

Another difficulty ladies experience when playing the in and out system is this business of retreating from the net. Again something they are not used to doing in mixed doubles. You must appreciate that as soon as your side put the shuttle into the air, you cannot afford to remain in a front and back formation. The lady at the back simply cannot cope on her own—indeed nor can a man in the mixed game—if the shuttle is constantly being lifted. Take the case where your team is on the attack and you are in the net position. All well and good whilst you keep the shuttle going down, but as soon as either of you clears it, you are giving the enemy a chance to smash—and their obvious target is you! In the net area you are very vulnerable to a smash and so you must get away from there with all speed into a sound defensive formation. Don't look round to see which is the best way out, you haven't the time, just move. If you can manage it, retreat along the path farthest away from the hitter, i.e. the diagonal. If your clearance was only half court you are in trouble, and so it would help if you retire with your racket held up in front of you. In this way there is a good chance that you will be able to get your racket to the shuttle as it is smashed at you, though you certainly don't have time to make much of a stroke.

When you are at the back of the court in a long rally, with your partner at the net, your shots should be down (but not a full-out smash unless you are pretty sure of winning the point, because of your recovery). Try drop shots and half smashes. This is also another time when the round-the-head shots come into their own. If, in the main, you direct your downward shots towards the centre, you will narrow the angle of return, you may confuse the opponents as to who should go for it and you should make it more difficult for them to have you chasing all along the base line.

All these situations require practice as you are not used to them and this is particularly so if, in your club, the accent is on mixed doubles. Establish a partnership with another lady and work at the problems together; this is the only way to acquire the very clear understanding between you that is absolutely essential.

Because ladies do not generally have the power of men, you can get away with more high serving in ladies' doubles and if your low service is not producing the desired result, by all means serve high. Your lady opponent may smash but I very much doubt that she will have the power to produce an outright winner, *if the serve is high and falling on the back service line.* Don't forget the disguised services and some variation of direction too.

There is more room for clears in the ladies' game as well. A full length clear, right on to the base line, is quite a difficult shot for a lady to deal with. She would be unwise to smash it and all she can do is another clear or a drop shot— most probably a slow drop shot. So, if you are in doubt, play it safe and clear it. It is better to play a good length clear and live again than try a risky shot that will only run you deeper into trouble.

The greatest weakness in the ladies' game is to be found along the base line and most particularly in the deep backhand corner. An intelligent player will exploit this weakness. The difficulty of coping with this backhand corner will be minimised if you react quickly and prepare, when at the back of the court, to play all high shots with a forehand— and not a backhand—stroke whenever possible.

I have not mentioned the positions you should adopt to serve and to receive service. These will be dictated by what you have learned from the sections on men's and mixed doubles coupled with your own experience in the ladies' game.

Try to play as much ladies' doubles as possible and as much as the men in your club will permit. It is quite different from mixed and needs a lot of practice to perfect. Because of their inability to smash through the opposition, longer rallies often occur in ladies' doubles. It is therefore very important to be able to play consistently without unforced errors for long periods. And to do this, you must have the practice.

TO CONCLUDE

This is not the whole story, not by any means. I have tried to emphasise what I consider to be the important fundamentals for, as I travel around, I see so much talent which has been wasted because the fundamentals are missing.

Now that you have read this book I think you will appreciate that there is a great deal more to badminton than just bashing a bird about. There is a lot to learn if you want to become a top player, but you cannot learn it all at once. You must progress through easy stages and to make this progression requires not only constant practice, but thought as well. Think about the game and what you are doing, all the time.

Badminton is both a science and an art. It is one of the most physically demanding sports, yet requires great finesse and, at the top level, the mind of a master chess player. But it is not essential to have all these fine attributes in order to enjoy it.

That is the great beauty of badminton. It can be played by all ages amongst a wide range of people and they can all derive so much pleasure from the game, regardless of their ability. So, go ahead and enjoy yourself!

THE LAWS OF BADMINTON

as revised in the year 1939 and adopted by

THE INTERNATIONAL BADMINTON FEDERATION

Subsequently revised up-to-date

COURT

1. (a) The Court shall be laid out as in the following Diagram 'A' (except in the case provided for in paragraph (b) of this Law) and to the measurements there shown, and shall be defined preferably by white or yellow lines, or, if this is not possible, by other easily distinguishable lines, $1\frac{1}{2}$ inches wide.

In marking the court, the width ($1\frac{1}{2}$ inches) of the centre lines shall be equally divided between the right and left service courts; the width ($1\frac{1}{2}$ inches each) of the short service line and the long service line shall fall within the 13-feet measurement given as the length of the service court; and the width ($1\frac{1}{2}$ inches each) of all other boundary lines shall fall within the measurements given.

(b) Where space does not permit of the marking out of a court for doubles, a court may be marked out for singles only as also shown in Diagram 'A'. The back boundary lines become also the long service lines, and the posts, or the strips of material representing them as referred to in Law 2, shall be placed on the side lines.

POSTS

2. The posts shall be 5 feet 1 inch in height from the floor. They shall be sufficiently firm to keep the net strained as provided in Law 3, and shall be placed on the side boundary lines of the court. Where this is not practicable, some method must be employed for indicating the position of the side boundary line where it passes under the net, e.g. by the use of a thin post or strip of material, not less than $1\frac{1}{2}$ inches in width, fixed to the side boundary line and rising vertically to the net cord. Where this is in use on a court marked for doubles it shall be placed on the boundary line of the doubles court irrespective of whether singles or doubles are being played.

NET

3. The net shall be made of fine tanned cord of from $\frac{5}{8}$ inch to $\frac{3}{4}$ inch mesh. It shall be firmly stretched from post to post, and shall be 2 feet 6 inches in depth. The top of the net shall be 5 feet in height from the floor at the centre, and 5 feet 1 inch at the posts, and shall be edged with a 3 inch white tape doubled and supported by a cord or cable run through the tape and strained over and flush with the top of the posts.

SHUTTLE

4. A shuttle shall weigh from 73 to 85 grains, and shall have from 14 to 16 feathers fixed in a cork, 1 inch to 1⅛ inches in diameter. The feathers shall be from 2½ to 2¾ inches in length from the tip to the top of the cork base. They shall have from 2⅛ to 2½ inches spread at the top and shall be firmly fastened with thread or other suitable material.

Subject to there being no substantial variation in the general design, pace, weight and flight of the shuttle, modifications in the above specifications may be made, subject to the approval of the National Organisation concerned.

(a) in places where atmospheric conditions, due either to altitude or climate, make the standard shuttle unsuitable; or

(b) if special circumstances exist which make it otherwise expedient in the interests of the game.

(*The Badminton Association of England has approved the use of modified shuttles (e.g. plastic, nylon, etc.), for play in England.*)

A shuttle shall be deemed to be of correct pace if, when a player of average strength strikes it with a full underhand stroke from a spot immediately above one back boundary line in a line parallel to the side lines, and at an upward angle, it falls not less than 1 foot, and not more than 2 feet 6 inches short of the other back boundary line.

PLAYERS

5. (a) The word 'Player' applies to all those taking part in a game.

(b) The game shall be played, in the case of the doubles game, by two players a side, and in the case of the singles game, by one player a side.

(c) The side for the time being having the right to serve shall be called the 'In' side, and the opposing side shall be called the 'Out' side.

THE TOSS

6. Before commencing play the opposing sides shall toss, and the side winning the toss shall have the option of:

(a) Serving first; or

(b) Not serving first; or

(c) Choosing ends.

The side losing the toss shall then have choice of any alternative remaining.

SCORING

7. (a) The doubles and men's singles game consists of 15 or 21 points. as may be arranged. Provided that in a game of 15 points, when the score is 13-all, the side which first reached 13 has the option of 'Setting' the game to 5, and that when the score is 14-all, the side which first reached 14 has the option of 'Setting' the game to 3. After the game has been 'Set' the score is called 'Love All', and the side which first scores 5 or 3 points, according as the game has been 'Set' at 13-or 14-all, wins the game. In either case the claim to 'Set' the game must be made before the next service is delivered after the score has reached 13-all or 14-all. Provided also that in a game of 21 points the same method of scoring be adopted, substituting 19 and 20 for 13 and 14.

(b) The ladies' singles game consists of 11 points. Provided that when the score is '9-all' the player who first reached 9 has the option of 'Setting' the game to 3, and when the score is '10-all' the player who first reached 10 has the option of 'Setting' the game to 2.

(c) A side rejecting the option of 'Setting' at the first opportunity shall not be thereby barred from 'Setting' if a second opportunity arises.

(d) In handicap games 'Setting' is not permitted.

8. The opposing sides shall contest the best of three games, unless otherwise agreed. The players shall change ends at the commencement of the second game and also of the third game (if any). In the third game the players shall change ends when the leading score reaches:

(a) 8 in a game of 15 points;
(b) 6 in a game of 11 points;
(c) 11 in a game of 21 points;

or, in handicap events, when one of the sides has scored half the total number of points required to win the game (the next highest number being taken in case of fractions). When it has been agreed to play only one game the players shall change ends as provided above for the third game.

If, inadvertently, the players omit to change ends as provided in this Law at the score indicated, the ends shall be changed immediately the mistake is discovered, and the existing score shall stand.

DOUBLES PLAY

9. (a) It having been decided which side is to have the first service, the player in the right-hand service court of that side commences the game by serving to the player in the service court diagonally opposite. If the latter player returns the shuttle before it touches the ground it is to be returned by one of the 'In' side, and then returned by one of the 'Out'

side, and so on, until a fault is made or the shuttle ceases to be 'In Play'. (*Vide* paragraph (b).) If a fault is made by the 'In' side, its right to continue serving is lost, as only one player on the side beginning a game is entitled to do so (*vide* Law 11), and the opponent in the right-hand service court then becomes the server; but if the service is not returned, or the fault is made by the 'Out' side, the 'In' side scores a point. The 'In' side players then change from one service court to the other, the service now being from the left-hand service court to the player in the service court diagonally opposite. So long as a side remains 'In' service is delivered alternately from each service court into the one diagonally opposite, the change being made by the 'In' side when, and only when, a point is added to its score.

(b) The first service of a side in each innings shall be made from the right-hand service court. A 'Service' is delivered as soon as the shuttle is struck by the server's racket. The shuttle is thereafter 'In Play' until it touches the ground, or until a fault or 'Let' occurs, or except as provided in Law 19. After the service is delivered, the server and the player served to may take up any positions they choose on their side of the net, irrespective of any boundary lines.

10. The player served to may alone receive the service, but should the shuttle touch, or be struck by, his partner the 'In' side scores a point. No player may receive two consecutive services in the same game, except as provided in Law 12.

11. Only one player of the side beginning a game shall be entitled to serve in its first innings. In all subsequent innings each partner shall have the right, and they shall serve consecutively. The side winning a game shall always serve first in the next game, but either of the winners may serve and either of the losers may receive the service.

12. If a player serves out of turn, or from the wrong service court (owing to a mistake as to the service court from which service is at the time being in order), *and his side wins the rally*, it shall be a 'Let' provided that such 'Let' be claimed or allowed before the next succeeding service is delivered.

If a player standing in the wrong service court takes the service, *and his side wins the rally*, it shall be a 'Let', provided that such 'Let' be claimed or allowed before the next succeeding service is delivered.

If in either of the above cases the side at fault *loses the rally*, the mistake shall stand and the players' positions shall not be corrected during the remainder of that game.

DIAGRAM (A)
Doubles Court
Diagonal Measurement of full Court: 48 ft. 4 in.
Diagonal Measurement of half Court: 29 ft. 8¾ in.
(from post to back boundary line).

Singles Court
Diagonal Measurement of full court: 47 ft. 2 in.
Diagonal Measurement of half Court: 27 ft. 9⅝ in.
(from post to back boundary line).

Should a player inadvertently change sides when he should not do so, and the mistake not be discovered until after the next succeeding service has been delivered, the mistake shall stand, and a 'Let' cannot be claimed or allowed, and the players' positions shall not be corrected during the remainder of that game.

SINGLES PLAY

13. In singles Laws 9 and 12 hold good, except that:

    (a) The players shall serve from and receive service in their respective right-hand service courts only when the server's score is 0 or an even number of points in the game, the service being delivered from and received in their respective left-hand service courts when the server's score is an odd number of points.

    (b) Both players shall change service courts after each point has been scored.

FAULTS

14. A fault made by a player of the side which is 'In' puts the server out; if made by a player whose side is 'Out', it counts a point to the 'In' side.

    It is a fault:

    (a) If, in serving, the shuttle at the instant of being struck be higher than the server's waist, or if any part of the head of the racket, at the instant of striking the shuttle, be higher than any part of the server's hand holding the racket.

    (b) If, in serving, the shuttle falls into the wrong service court (i.e. into the one not diagonally opposite to the server), or falls short of the short service line, or beyond the long service line, or outside the side boundary lines of the service court into which service is in order.

    (c) If the server's feet are not in the service court from which service is at the time being in order, or if the feet of the player receiving the service are not in the service court diagonally opposite until the service is delivered. (*Vide* Law 16.)

    (d) If before or during the delivery of the service any player makes preliminary feints or otherwise intentionally baulks his opponent.

    (e) If either in service or play, the shuttle falls outside the boundaries of the court, or passes through or under the net, or fails to pass the net, or touches the roof or side walls, or the person or dress of a player. (A shuttle falling on a line shall be deemed to have fallen in the court or service court of which such line is a boundary.)

    (f) If the shuttle 'In Play' be struck before it crosses to the striker's side of the net. (The striker may, however, follow the shuttle over the net with his racket in the course of his stroke.)

(g) If, when the shuttle is 'In Play', a player touches the net or its support with racket, person or dress.

(h) If the shuttle be held on the racket (i.e. caught or slung) during the execution of a stroke; or if the shuttle be hit twice in succession by the same player with two strokes; or if the shuttle be hit by a player and his partner successively.

(i) If, in play, a player strikes the shuttle (unless he thereby makes a good return) or is struck by it, whether he is standing within or outside the boundaries of the court.

(j) If a player obstructs an opponent.

(k) If Law 16 be transgressed.

GENERAL

15. The server may not serve till his opponent is ready, but the opponent shall be deemed to be ready if a return of the service be attempted.

16. The server and the player served to must stand within the limits of their respective courts (as bounded by the short and long service, the centre, and side lines), and some part of both feet of these players must remain in contact with the ground in a stationary position until the service is delivered. A foot on or touching a line in the case of either the server or the receiver shall be held to be outside his service court. (*Vide* Law 14(c).) The respective partners may take up any position, provided they do not unsight or otherwise obstruct an opponent.

17(a) If in the course of service or rally, the shuttle touches and passes over the net, the stroke is not invalidated thereby. It is a good return if the shuttle having passed outside either post drops on or within the boundary lines of the opposite court. A 'Let' may be given by the umpire for any unforeseen or accidental hindrance.

(b) If, in service, or during a rally, a shuttle, *after passing over the net, is caught in or on the net*, it is a 'Let'.

(c) If the receiver is faulted for moving before the service is delivered, or for not being within the correct service court, in accordance with Laws 14(c) or 16, and at the same time the server is also faulted for a service infringement, it shall be a let.

(d) When a 'Let' occurs, the play since the last service shall not count, and the player who served shall serve again, except when Law 12 is applicable.

18. If the server, in attempting to serve, misses the shuttle, it is not a fault; but if the shuttle be touched by the racket, a service is thereby delivered.

19. If when in play, the shuttle strikes the net and remains suspended there, or strikes the net and falls towards the ground on the striker's side of the net, or hits the ground outside the court and an opponent then touches the net or shuttle with his racket or person, there is no penalty, as the shuttle is not *then* in play.

20. If a player has a chance of striking the shuttle in a downward direction when quite near the net, his opponent must not put up his racket near the net on the chance of the shuttle rebounding from it. This is obstruction within the meaning of Law 14(j).

A player may, however, hold up his racket to protect his face from being hit if he does not thereby baulk his opponent.

21. It shall be the duty of the umpire to call 'Fault' or 'Let' should either occur, without appeal being made by the players, and to give his decision on any appeal regarding a point in dispute, if made before the next service; and also to appoint linesmen and service judges at his discretion. The umpire's decision shall be final, but he shall uphold the decision of a linesman or service judge. This shall not preclude the umpire also from faulting the server or receiver. Where, however, a referee is appointed, an appeal shall lie to him from the decision of an umpire on questions of law only.

CONTINUOUS PLAY

22. Play shall be continuous from the first service until the match be concluded; except that (a) in the International Badminton Championship and in the Ladies' International Badminton Championship there shall be allowed an interval not exceeding five minutes between the second and third games of a match; (b) in countries where climatic conditions render it desirable, there shall be allowed, subject to the previously published approval of the National Organisation concerned, an interval not exceeding five minutes between the second and third games of a match, in singles or doubles, or both; and (c) when necessitated by circumstances not within the control of the players, the umpire may suspend play for such a period as he may consider necessary. If play be suspended the existing score shall stand and play be resumed from that point. Under no circumstances shall play be suspended to enable a player to recover his strength or wind, or to receive instruction or advice. Except in the case of any interval already provided for above, no player shall be allowed to receive advice during a match or to leave the court until the match be concluded without the umpire's consent. The umpire shall be the sole judge of any suspension of play and he shall have the right to disqualify any offender.

(*The Badminton Association of England has not sanctioned any interval between the second and third games of a match.*)

INTERPRETATIONS

1. Any movement or conduct by the server that has the effect of breaking the continuity of service after the server and receiver have taken their positions to serve and to receive the service is a preliminary feint.
(*Vide* Law 14(d).)

2. It is obstruction if a player invades an opponent's court with racket or person in any degree except as permitted in Law 14(f).
(*Vide* Law 14(j).)

3. Where necessary on account of the structure of a building, the local Badminton Authority may, subject to the right of veto of its National Organisation, make bye-laws dealing with cases in which a shuttle touches an obstruction.